*There should be an African Dream; A Dream of Societies of Opportunities Where every youth would be Physically, Mentally and Spiritually equipped To create Wealth, Grow their societies, And sustain the Societies for future Generations.*

*A Dream of a Continent where you can become whatever you aspire to be, as long as you have the Skills and Ambition.*

*Africa should be a Mother providing education, jobs, security, and protection for all her Youth for them to secure fulfilment in their lives and acquire happiness.*

Published by      :  NYAMEAMA Publications
Printed by        :  CreateSpace
Book Design by  :  Dennis Amoah Antwi
Edited by         :  Wendy Linda Osei Akoto
Cover Design    :  Ernest Nkrumah Taylor

ISBN-10 : 1501022911
ISBN-13 : 978-1501022913

AVAILABLE FROM:

Amazon and Other Online / Book Stores
And on Kindle and Other devices.


**email:** arnoldboateng@gmail.com

# TABLE OF CONTENTS

## CHAPTER 4

## POLICY ISSUES RELATIVE TO YOUR DREAMS

## CHAPTER 5

## CHAPTER 9

# CHAPTER 10

# CHAPTER 11

# CHAPTER 12

## CHAPTER 13

### YOUTH ENTREPRENEURSHIP, APPRENTICESHIP AND VOLUNTEERISM...................................................................**166**

## CHAPTER 14

## CHAPTER 15

## CHAPTER 16

## DEDICATION

*To the African Youth;*

*And youth leaders in politics, academia, business, and ALL*

*To the African youth;*

*That she would grow into the new society: viable, resourceful and healthy;*

*A society able to meet her needs as she aspires and strives for the African dream;*

*A dream of Societies of equal opportunities, abundance and prosperity,*

*A society where you can become whatever you want to be;*

*Nations defined by Ideas and stabilised by compassion, personal freedoms, honesty, love, hard work, fairness and contentment;*

*And not by material wealth, greed, depravity, hatred, ethnicity or colour;*

*The Lands of Gold*

## ACKNOWLEDGEMENT

To the LORD GOD ALMIGHTY for the strength, energy and favour I enjoyed throughout the preparation of this book. I also express my warmest appreciation to the helpers He brought my way.

Special thanks go to the Youth in Africa, who through their wonderful initiatives, have given me the hope that, a New and Better Africa is being born; we have a Future as long as the youth continue to dream and work hard.

To Kwasi Frimpong, NEDIA Africa, for his structuring and recommendations on the Policy Dimension section of the book;

To Sefakor Gohoho, a Pan African Entrepreneur, for her wits and bold suggestions;

To Ernest Taylor and David Charway for the cover design;

To Wendy Linda Wordie for editorial and proofreading the work;

To the unseen persons who supported me in all manner of ways;

To all who participated in the prayer sessions for this work;

To Samuel Nsiah, my Personal Assistant;

And to Ohene Djan for his suggestions on youth orientation and outlook;

To the Hon. Opare-Ansah, Member of Parliament for Suhum, Ghana, and a member of the ECOWAS Parliament who gave me office space in the last few months of this work;

To my Wife for her support and Son for his sacrifices and inspiration;

To The SOVEREIGN LORD be Glory and Honour.

## INTRODUCTION

*Beginnings*

It is time for Africa to be the continent where dreams are born, nurtured and realised; a continent where the hopeless and destitute find their path. It is time to educate our youth, broaden their horizon and create opportunities for them. Africa can and should be the beacon of light for our youth in a world where many young persons have become restless and apprehensive.

There is no doubt that, many of the African youth are liberated in their minds, horizon, dreams and ambitions. Many of you are dreaming again and working hard to achieve your dreams. Your self-belief and confidence is overwhelming. Many of you have now understood and embraced the 'I can do' attitude.

Across the continent, you are educating yourselves to the highest levels. In many cases, you are doing so through private education to acquire the skills to tap into the limited opportunities around. Others are also innovating to create their own opportunities.

For the first time in many decades, *entrepreneurship* has caught your attention and imagination. The African society is filled with an energetic youth, who is ambitious, educated and provides the ready and necessary workforce for developmental push.

Without question, your greatest unspeakable obstacle is the political elite and their bedfellows. What foundation and legacy is the political elite leaving for the youth? The political elite needs to answer this question or the youth should find an appropriate means to elicit a response.

The 21st Century could easily be the century for the African youth, if politicians would pursue the right policies and support programmes which would help you to acquire the needed character, knowledge and skills to tap into the enormous opportunities it offers. This calls for the African politicians to create an environment where basic skills, ambition and the right attitude on the part of the youth would be enough to earn a job and make a decent living.

On the part of the African youth, this century could be your century if you would dream again, challenge the status quo and acquire the needed attitudes and skills inherent in making you useful to yourself and society.

If you are in school or learning a trade, or working as a young professional, consider that you have a role in determining your future.

You are not expected to be a politician in order to contribute to the creation of opportunities or be part of the political process. Your role is to contribute to professional and policy discussions, and implementation of the same by virtue of your social, cultural or professional endeavours.

In other words, it is important for you to strenuously make input into policy and national development. Without such an effort, there is no way you could genuinely affect policy and steer the resources of state towards your development.

Nothing would come on a silver platter nor would politicians and policy makers get up one day to commit themselves to making the youth agenda a number one national priority without a deliberate, conscious and religious effort on the part of the youth. As such, the 'African youth must put pressure' on their leaders. It is a competition for attention and a share of the national cake; the loudest and consistent 'pusher' gets attention.

It is necessary to ensure that, you either take part in the political process directly or encourage like-minded persons to champion your cause. This notwithstanding, there is the need to demand accountability and feedback from people you so elect or put forward to push your cause.

Governments must prioritise areas of need and must be prepared to spend enormous resources on the priority areas. The 21$^{st}$ century favours certain job markets more than others. For example, information technology and its related programmes such as computer programming, system analysis and software development cut across most sectors of economies and industries and as a result offer more employment opportunities. By way of example, governments should make it a policy to train more of its next generation of youth in ICT and computer languages.

Beyond training, governments ought to create the environment for ICT businesses to thrive so that, the youth would be able to secure jobs after training. On the other hand, entrepreneurially attuned youth ought to be supported to start their own businesses, grow them and create employment in the larger economy.

You can readily make it as you dream. It is your thoughts, determination and your will to succeed which would pave the way and become that 'creative force' which has helped many dreamers to achieve their dreams. In the absence of positive thinking and attitude, no number of opportunities would be able to lift you up to your dreams.

At the end of the day, whatever dreams so conceived, it is very much affected by the political environment within your respective societies. As such, it is naïve on the part of those of you who refuse to follow the political process or make inputs into it to conclude that, you are immune from policy decisions. The political process has enormous influence on your dreams by virtue of the position of politicians to control the resources of the state.

I do not expect all of you to be politicians. My advice is that, follow the events in your societies. Attend meetings and make your opinions heard. Read the newspapers and take part in advocacy.

I encourage you to pursue a better future. A future which would bestow on you opportunities for prosperity and better living conditions: good drinking water, secured jobs, education, dignity and respect among your peers worldwide. Sincerely, such a future can forever be a pipe dream if politicians do not support you with the right policies and programmes.

Do not take it for granted that you would wake up one day to have abundance of opportunities; not at all. Your leaders would have to make deliberate decisions to create the opportunilties for you. Furthermore, they should have the political will to implement those policies.

The future of every society is tied to the quality of its youth. The United Nations in its World Programme of Action agrees in letter that, 'the imagination, ideals and energies of young people are vital for the continuing development of the societies in which they live'. Your contributions are key to the lifelong continuity of the nation.

If you pursue politicians for accountability and make constructive suggestions towards right policies and programmes, then I can assure you that, you may have the needed environment and opportunities in achieving your dreams.

## *You Need the Right Environment*

Most of our societies have become barren lands for many of our youth.

The African youth is at the cross-road. You either rise up to the leaders for better environment or you would be left behind. Your colleagues in the Far East, Mainland Asia, Brazil and around the world are moving forward. It is your right to move forward and achieve your dreams.

You are in different times. You have better tools. You should learn from the failures of your fathers. You have the opportunity to be better. You are in new times and a new age with glorious benefits. Allow time to sweep away the evils and misplaced resources we wasted through unbridled materialism, lack of self-esteem and cowardice. The unbridled looting and greed of many a political leaders which is a short term gain for them, their families and close associates, is a long-term loss to the youth and the nation at large.

Eventually, we are all losers. As such, it is important for all to rise up and demand accountability from political and elected leaders before bitterness and rancour set in for us to tear one another apart. Social exclusion, poverty and inequality have been the root causes to many a conflict across the world.

## This is your time

The time has come for the African youth to stand up.

This is the time for the African youth to stand up and pursue their dreams without limitations to their rise. This is the time for the African youth to rise up and aspire to achieve great feats in the areas of Science, Mathematics, Architecture, and Music. There is no limit. Every obstacle could be overcome. Every hurdle must be surmounted. Every mental chain shall be broken and doors of opportunities burst open; be it geographic, mental or psychological. This is your time. You carry the genes of greatness.

## POLITICAL DIMENSION OF ISSUES

*'Politics is war without bloodshed while war is politics with bloodshed'*

Mao Tse-Tung (Mao Zedong), commonly referred to as Chairman Mao (December 26th, 1893 – September 9th, 1976). He was a Chinese Communist Revolutionary, Guerrilla Warfare Strategist, Poet, Political Philosopher, and Leader of the Chinese Revolution. He was the architect and founding Father of the People's Republic of China.

*'Fortune favours the Bold'*

# 1

## Are the Political Elites the Enemy?

*"A leader is one who ventures and takes the risks of going out ahead to show the way and whom others follow, voluntarily, because they are persuaded that the leader's path is the right one – for them, probably better than they could devise for themselves."*

Robert Greenleaf (1904 – 1990), Management Theorist and Author

The *African Youth Decade (2009 - 2018) Plan Of Action*, adopted on the 26th of July, 2006 in Banjul, which is supposed to be one of the legal framework guiding member states to implement targets meant to create opportunities for the youth, has been ratified by only twenty-four members out of the fifty-three-membership Union. Its lofty objectives do not have much to show on the ground as member states strangely drag their feet.

Clearly it seems the plan died in Banjul before it reached other capitals. Besides South Africa, Ghana, Kenya, Rwanda, Ethiopia and some few others where reasonable progress could be seen, largely most countries are silent on the *action* part of the plan or do not have meaningful youth employment programmes in considerable relation to the large army of unemployed youth on the continent?

Suffice to say, there are glimpses of hope dotted around our nations. Burkina Faso has the Youth Development and Skills Development Project, Cameroun has the Tabitha, Ethiopia has the Youth Venture Initiative, Kenya has the Agri-Trade Kenya and over hundred other programmes, South Africa has over six programmes including Umsobomvu Youth Fund, Tunisia has Souk At-tanmia initiative for young entrepreneurs. In Morocco, there is the Provision Matching Grants for enhancing employability of young graduates. Rwanda has the Skills Employability and Entrepreneurship Programme (SEEP) and Ghana has the Ghana Youth Employment and Entrepreneurial Development Agency (GYEEDA).

In 2013, Ethiopia launched a twenty-six million dollar ($26m) initiative: Entrepreneurship Development Programme (EDP) in partnership with the United Nations to support a broad -based entrepreneurship scheme.

Even though it does not specifically target the youth, the youth is not excluded either. It is hoped that, with a target of empowering two hundred thousand people by 2015, large number of the youth could get into the scheme.

On the continental level, on the 12th of September 2013, the African Union Commission, in Addis Ababa, signed the *Joint Initiative on Youth Employment in Africa* (JYEIA) as a follow-up to the Malabo and Ouagadougou declarations and Action Plans. We all hope for real time concrete results from these commitments as a realistic means of addressing the African youth question. Already, many commentators have begun predicting many states unravelling from youth implosion. If hope is enough, which I doubt in this instance, then let us hope it does not come to that.

The challenge for Africa is not the matter of lack of policies or programmes for that matter. Among the African nations assessed by the United Nations Multi-Donor Trust Fund, there are nearly two hundred and fifty (250) different youth programmes on the continent. These exclude programmes run by NGOs and Civil Society groups. The challenge is more about:

1. Promoting the right and smart policies in a context relevant to national policy direction and aspirations of the youth.

2. Adequate and timely review of existing programmes.

3. Researching, adopting and localising success stories around the world.

4. Capacity of policy makers to design policies to meet the needs of the youth.

5. Political will on the part of political leaders to follow through with promises and take risks.

6. National Coordination of programmes among government institutions to share experiences and lessons.

7. Capacity of programme managers. Often management goes to political loyalist and cronies without any tough assessment of their technical expertise relative to the programme.

8. Political interference has normally prevented technocrats from pursuing the programmes in the context of established timelines.

9. Political Election cycles.

The United Nations (UNCDF) YouthStart Initiative in partnership with The MasterCard Foundation is a promising initiative which ought to be watched closely. The Initiative seeks to provide savings and financial education to the youth in Sub-Saharan Africa. Even though its capacity is far away from the about ten million jobs required annually for the continent, it adds to the other efforts by governments and other institutions.

## Is it a matter of Sarcasm or Hypocrisy?

Consider the opening paragraph of the foreword to Plan of Action. It reads:

> *'Imagine that the youth in Africa is able to effectively contribute and benefit from Africa's renewal and lives Africa's dream of prosperity, peace, stability and in charge of its own destiny'*

How lofty and uplifting. Yet beyond these inspiring words, there is not much to show on the ground towards a more meaningful course of empowering the African Youth to survive the coming decades and /or meeting the extremely modest objectives set out in the many action plans. Is there much concrete steps taken to achieve the prosperity, peace and stability set out in the objectives of the action plan?

How can the youth contribute to Africa's renewal when large sections of them have no skills, education and above all, confidence to approach life in its wholeness? How can there be prosperity when leaders have become greedy looters and intellectuals have betrayed their course and have thus sold themselves over for perks and loot? It is painful to observe how far many of the leaders have departed from their own action plans, policies and programmes and the welfare of our youth.

How most African leaders intend to achieve prosperity for their youth is also yet to be seen and appraised on the continental level.

The overriding issue of youth unemployment which is causing unrest and apprehension among the active youth and section of the policy fraternity is yet to be addressed fully either in policy or by sustainable programmes. Sadly, it seems most of our leaders and their governments have no realistic sense of tomorrow or the urgency of these times.

The *African Youth Question* is a time bomb waiting to explode. The World Bank estimates that, 11 million African youth are expected to join the labour market each year for the next ten years. Other researchers put the figure between 7-10million. Whichever of the estimates you choose does not make the situation less alarming. The job market for the African youth is dire, notwithstanding the high uneven growth rates (GDP) reported by many countries.

Not surprisingly, many an African youth have come to regard many of our leaders as the stumbling block to their dreams; the great 'evil' serving as the barrier to their aspirations, hope and the promise of a better future.

Yes, many of our youth consider the political establishment as the *enemy*. It is my hope that tomorrow, this characterisation could change from *'the enemy'* to *'the friend'*. I dare say that, this could only happen when the questions of skills training and employment opportunities are tackled head-on in a manner devoid of political positioning, propaganda and vote canvassing.

Suffice to say, an equally important message goes to you the youth and youth leaders, to take note of your respective roles in order to create a balance between your demands and your responsibilities. This awareness would help you to contribute meaningfully to national development in a manner devoid of bitterness, hopelessness and anger.

You should also take note of your responsibility to urge politicians to put in place and support the right programmes.

Political leadership ought to win the confidence of the youth with concrete programmes instead of promises. The African political leadership needs to prove to the youth that, their interests are paramount, and thus, they are supporting job creation and their aspirations.

Many of our societies have come to associate most politicians with the failure and breakdown of institutions. Promises made are never kept. Threats, coercion and buyouts are used to silence voices and plough to political office. Businesses are attacked on the perception of being receptive to opposition political parties. Representatives of the people dabble and trade in dubious endeavours. Some swindle and commit acts bordering on outright criminality.

Your generation is wiser. You no longer believe that, the current poor state of many of our societies is the sole work of *The West* or some forces outside your shores. You are very much aware of the apathy and 'con' of some political leaders. You should also be aware that, political leaders have the capacity and resources to create an environment which would create jobs and offer opportunities needed for you to meet your aspirations.

Use your intellectual capacity to read and interpret budget statements and to discern resources allocations and strongly put your views forward. Send the message out that, it is time for politicians to demonstrate to you that you can go to bed in peace knowing that they are planning and working for your welfare and *The Future*. It is your right and it is their duty to provide that right. Yes, it is time for African leaders to prove to the African youth that, they can put their minds to rest because they are planning and working for their welfare by fighting corruption, supporting youth programmes, halting the looting and serving as the solid bedrock of protection and security for an apprehensive youth.

## Guilty On the Moral Front

On the moral front, though none the better, political leadership has a bigger role in setting the standards. On this front too, most of them have undoubtedly failed. The big picture is that, the failure of leadership influences youth development and other key areas of society. It is perhaps this failure which has resulted in the massive lack of empathy on the path of many leaders and the consequent invincibility of corruption and looting.

Political leadership has enormous control in the society. They control budgets and resources of the state; they exercise constitutional and coercive powers and they partly set the agenda for the media. For this reason, it is important to stress the need for exemplary leadership and accountability on the part of political leaders.

## Political Role in Developing a Progressive Environment

The role of political leadership in the creation and development of a viable and progressive environment is key to your development and aspirations. This is partly as a result of the roles of political leadership in policy formulation, direction and control over national resources. The actions and (or) flaws of political leaders are thus, critical in ensuring that the society charts a good course for your future sustenance or otherwise.

## Are Politicians The Stumbling Block to Your Development?

There is a nagging and painful perception that, politicians are the enemies of society. Thus, some leaders are the stumbling block between our nations and the promise of wealth and prosperous societies. This may not be entirely truthful in all cases, but the society believes it and it has gained currency.

Political leadership should be characterised by responsibility to their constituencies. When called upon to honour their obligations, they must not regard such call as annoyance; rather, it should be seen as an honour and a religious duty to do so. They should take pride and fulfilment in the fact that they have provided safe drinking water, an efficient health care system, security for life and property, effective justice system and other institutions inherent in ensuring a habitable society.

It is in this light that the constituents which so elect leaders would find the political process a big partner in peace and development. Thus, the political class should show leadership by taking the headway on major issues reflective of our aspirations and values as a society.

May the African youth gather the strength and courage to say to the politicians that, 'we believed in ourselves once; make us believe...again'. Make the youth believe in a dream of a better Africa and prosperous community of nations again. Make us believe that, our potentials are unlimited. And that, in Mother Africa, the youth would find security, harmony and strength to build a continent of opportunities and hope for all who dream and aspire to the liberating light of development and prosperity which would lift the society out of poverty and bring fulfilment and happiness to the continent.

Let's believe again. Let's believe in the dreams of Nkrumah, Father Nyerere, Steve Biko, Antha Diop, and Sadat. Let us believe in the voice of peace, prosperity, and love. For in these, we would defeat the vices which are plaguing our beloved continent and set ourselves free towards prosperity and wealth which shall not be overshadowed by inequality.

### Attitude of Leaders Affect You

The youth observe the environment and pick values from it more than they would read or learn from school or literature. So the actions of political leaders should reflect their titles as 'Honourable' men and 'Excellencies'. Their actions should echo the higher values of our society. Politicians are to show leadership by exerting influence positively, setting priorities to meet the basic need of the youth whilst showing integrity in their manners and character.

Furthermore, showing good attitude and calmness, vision and servitude to the course of the youth and larger society in their quests and aspirations is a mark of realistic inclination towards the youth. Largely, political leadership's support for the youth is made known when they (national, regional, zonal and religious) draw up policies, which support the interests of the youth. It is an essential necessity to bear in mind that, the aspirations, dreams, circumstances and abilities of the various sections of the youth are central to the prosperity of every nation.

There should be no second-guessing on the part of any government when it comes to youth policies and programmes. Government has an important role in not only enacting a coherent youth policy; rather, they should go beyond and implement such policies without discriminations based upon political affiliations, ethnicity and class.

In the pursuit of these policies and programmes, it is important to note and acknowledge the role of other stakeholders such as the clergy, youth activists, and civil society. Often, the pattern has been to get consultants together to draft stereotyped policies with tangential statistics and spiral projections as a policy to guide youth programmes. Such detached means of making policy are no longer effective.

Broad-based participation in such endeavours is the way forward. Such approaches broaden the appeal of any such policy and consequently its success. Mass participation from the grass root is a fundamental prerequisite for the success of policies and programmes. Most importantly, and perhaps for the audience of this book, the youth constituency should be included in the development of the political environment for the purposes of grooming them and secondly for their progressive integration into the society.

Specific to the youth, two dimensions need consideration. On one hand, those educated with higher needs; living in urban centres and cities and, on the other hand, those in villages, with barely any form of formal education craving for existential needs. These two groups crave for separate development needs and solutions. Despite this fact, there is a common need between them, thus, both need leadership (an avenue for real direction) and support for self-development.

It is important to observe that, political leadership has roles to play beyond making promises and failing to honour them.

In your advocacy, beyond specific national issues, which you must offer an opinion on, broadly, you should note three areas politicians ought to take a central role. These are:

1. Creating the right environment that would support the dreams of the youth; an environment which would offer them the right opportunities to aspire, and dream of heights as would his counterpart in any part of the world. This could be done using a road map such as national youth policy with concrete programmes and adequate resources to support the programmes.

2. Secondly, it is the duty of political leadership to provide resources, nurture, grow, and support this environment to serve its primary purpose of supporting the youth in their endeavours under all conceivable conditions and times. That is to say, there should be institutions to implement youth policies. These institutions should be supported with the adequate resources and personnel. In this light, the personnel should be selected on a competitive basis using best practice. They should operate without undue political influences. Once the sticky hands of politicians set in, they would lose their focus and balance. Or better, governments should support civil society and /or private institutions to extend their activities and expand the same in reaching out to the youth to take over large sections of the youth question.

3. Finally, political leadership has a solemn duty to protect this environment from attack, threats, and to ensure that nothing prevents the institutions of state from serving their primary purpose. The youth and other

stakeholders should be consulted regularly on the progress of the road map. Additionally, there should be a regular review of the youth policy to make sure that, it is relevant to the aspirations of the youth as technology and time alter many foundations.

## Showing Concern for the Youth

It is within the responsibilities above that, a government could be said to be concerned about the youth and be a friend. When such a government succeeds in this venture, it would not only have served the crying needs of the present generation of youth, but also those of generations to come.

The design and creation of structures to meet this goal is beyond political gain. It is far loftier than meeting campaign promises. It stabilises a nation. It guarantees rich grounds for nurturing and providing adequate growth for the youth who are being called to steer the craft of state.

Thus, the beauty of this venture is that there is an immediate gain of resourcing a huge human resource base which is encapsulated in the youth. It further goes to serve as a check to holding the youth back from engaging in delinquent actions: drugs, violence and other misdemeanours.

This environment should be diverse enough to support the many talents of the youth so that no one is cut out by design or lack of space in the environment. Rather, any youth cut off from our dreams as a nation should be as a result of his actions, faults and inadequacies and not for lack of opportunities or resources to succeed. There is no better avenue for a political leadership or government to serve the youth beyond creating a rich environment, and growing and nourishing the same.

14

## *Defining the Right Environment*

It is important to define the right environment in the context of government policy, youth aspirations and reality. What the youth may deem as the right environment may not necessarily reflect the ideology and policy inclinations of the political leadership. On the other hand, realities and conditions might not allow the dreams of the youth or the political directions of the ruling government to implement them. Nevertheless, the fact remains that, whatever the reality of policies and the economy, the government owes the youth a legitimate claim to build or improve the prevailing environment to meet their aspirations.

In creating the right environment, there is the need for certain basic processes and structures to be considered. This is of course, besides the technical issue of policy formulation, which usually includes the analysis of the problem and its environment, formulation of the policy and its implementation. In this vein, five suggestions are herein proposed:

1. The constitution of a National Youth Authority (NYA);

2. There should be an annual or periodic assembly of stakeholders including the youth (activists, student leadership, section of students), policy makers, educationists, counsellors, the clergy and others as the circumstance may allow, to periodically draft a new youth policy or review an existing policy or both with particular emphasis on skills acquisition, retraining, corrections, national orientation and response to emerging issues corresponding to patriotism, independence of thought, innovation, entrepreneurship and internationalization of ideas.

3. Definition of the progressive roles of the NYA with clear agenda, time lines, powers and deliverables. They should be set on the similar assessment scale as shareholders would to a Chief Executive or to a Board of Directors of a Limited Liability Company.

4. The NYA should be resourced to perform its functions favourably without political manipulation. Thus, the authority should be independent. It must have right over its policies, programme development, hiring of personnel, and its budget. (*Charged onto a Skills Development Levy*).

5. The NYA should work in consultation with international bodies with express interest in the affairs of the youth such as the African Union, the United Nation's Multi-Donor Trust Fund, Global Partnership for Youth Employment and International Youth Foundation, Plan International, and Youth Business International, among others, to harness their experience in delivering better services for the local youth.

The above, among others notwithstanding, are aimed at creating a working youth document. A smart national youth policy, which would lay down the foundation for the direction of youth development, create or expand the environment, correct the anomalies in the same, whilst sustaining the positive areas within the current environment.

Creating of a conducive environment is less romantic. It goes far beyond the making of policy. It calls for hard work, political capital, risks, painful trials and possible failures. In this endeavour, the loftiness of policy may definitely elude you.

The dynamic nature of the environment sought after, and the number of stakeholders involved denote that the institution ought to seriously liaise with stakeholders on a regular and continuous basis till the right environment is created. Thus, interactions are needed to ensure that the individual resources of these stakeholders are brought to bear on the sole goal of achieving a viable environment for the youth. The resultant society would be rich and tough enough to ensure that the youth going through it comes out with the right attitude, skills, and psychological orientations.

In the light of this, it is not difficult to ascertain the important role of an implementation institution.

### *Your Role as a Young Person In The Creation Of The Environment*

Could it be safely assumed that, you are aware of the important political responsibilities entrusted to you in the creation of a sustainable environment? Despite these assumptions, for the purposes of simplicity, I have itemised some key roles you ought to play towards the rich society you have for so long a time yearned for.

1.  Identify and work on the roles you are supposed to play and any other duty and obligation as mandated by the society and your profession religiously. You should be fit to perform the chosen duties based upon your skills. These duties are normally dynamic. That is to say, the fluid nature of the environment as a result of changing social, economic, political and technological trends requires that, you assess your roles periodically to reflect these changes.

2. Lend your support and services to the institutions, or any youth authority, individually or as body as in the case of youth groups or student unions in any way they are able.

3. Interact as well with other stakeholders within your societies to implement policies on the table.

4. You are expected to interact with your counterparts around the world so as to have a grasp of the issues and acquire new ideas.

5. Furthermore, you should learn continually to acquire knowledge and make constructive suggestions in the form of memos, position papers, and petitions among others, in the course of the process. Without lifelong education, you would not be effective in the long run.

6. You are to acquire skills in areas of lobbying and advocacy.

7. You ought to avoid actions and inactions, which would get in the way of the efforts of national youth institutions and other youth groups.

8. From the onset, you ought to take advantage of the opportunities created along the process of creating a rich environment. Additionally, you should endeavour to let the society see these benefits of your 'agitations' so as to justify any further demands required to complete and sustain the process of reforms. These

benefits should meet the open and intrinsic interests of the larger society.

9. Challenges within or created by the environment should be addressed through progressive dialogue. Dialogue usually takes time to resolve issues but the results are lasting and worth the labour and waiting.

10. You need to establish formal means of communication with concerned institutions and other relevant stakeholders.

11. You ought to forge unity among your ranks. Sometimes ego and ambition are the key challenges you face. Observing youth leaders, it is sometimes difficult to observe how you are often blinded by egos and unbridled ambitions. It is not a matter of who leads the efforts but how much you can achieve together in unity.

12. Do not allow yourselves either individually or as a collective body to be manipulated by 'big-men' or political institutions.

# 2

## Civil Society Organisations in Helping the Youth

*"Business, Labour and Civil Society organizations have skills and resources that are vital in helping to build a more robust global community."*

Kofi Annan (*Ghanaian Diplomat)* Seventh Secretary-General of the United Nations from 1st January 1997 – 31st December 2006; Nobel Peace Prize, 2001)

Civil Society has an important role to play in building and or sustaining a viable society for the youth. Their roles are as important as the roles of political leaders, or any other stakeholder. With tactfulness, capacity in policy and activism, civil society groups could be an avenue of resourcefulness for youth groups willing to influence policy and its implementation.

Thus:

1.  Civil society with its reach, expertise and vast network, could bring enormous pressure to bear on the political establishment to put the African Youth question top on the agenda. This should be a major project to get African leaders to commit themselves to set objectives. So far, the African Union and Regional Economic bloc's declarations have proven ineffective towards realizing their lofty goals in real terms. It is time to throw most of the leaders to the public and hold them accountable to their own pledges. Civil society's leadership is most welcome on this front.

2.  Provide guidance for the youth in the form of consultation and capacity building in advocacy.

3.  Conduct research work with the primary aim of identifying shifting orientation and ideological leanings among youth groups in order to influence policy in that direction.

4.  Nurture and protect cultural and moral values through advocacy by influencing policies, which would

21

strengthen cultural institutions. This will build and strengthen the youth to live up to their obligations and duties. Thus, amplify values such as compassion, humility and hard work and culture of our societies to the youth through regular interactions.

5.  Integrate the youth in their activities to give them space for their development in areas of advocacy and networking.

6.  As an independent body, civil society would have an advantage of neutrality on sensitive or hot button issues and bring to terms, the hard parts of government policies to the youth.

7.  In the pursuit of these roles, among others, it is important to be truthful to the youth when it comes to the realities of advocacy, which includes planning, dialogue and negotiations. That it takes real skills and patience to influence policies.

## Challenges for Civil Society Groups

In the pursuit of the lofty roles, there are real challenges Civil Society groups would have to contend with. These include:

1.  Institutional weakness and lack of adequate understanding of the role of Civil Societies in society.

2.  Inability of the youth to communicate in a clear understandable manner to Civil Society groups.

3.  Lack of resources for sustained campaigns to ensure substantive achievements.

4.  The dynamic nature of the environment calls for continual changes and adjustment, which Civil Society might not be up to speed with, due to funding constraints.

5.  Difficulty in coordinating the activities of student groups and interests because of unwillingness on the part of youth groups to engage each other. Sometimes, some of these youth leadership would be restless. At other times, some could be 'agents' of the political establishment.

6.  Flirting with political establishments, which sometimes affect their judgment, fairness and acceptability by sections of the youth.

7.  Change in youth leadership brings in new leaders who need fresh learning and a steep learning curve.

Nevertheless, it is important to acknowledge that, Civil Society on the continent is experienced enough to notice and overcome these challenges. With right motivation and resources, they could effectively lend a hand to the youth in building a coalition towards achieving their collective interests.

## The Art of Sustaining the Environment

The leadership roles in sustaining the environment should rest with the government, the youth, civil society and other stakeholders and not on any single institution or individual. The need to sustain the environment is necessary for a number of reasons. Notable among them is the continual development of the youth for a sustained national development drive. Secondly, without a viable environment, it would be virtually impossible to provide a sustained platform for the development of the youth. What use is education and skills if there are no opportunities to tap into?

Since the structures, conditions and resources towards the achievement of the dreams of the youth and national development are rooted in this environment, it is not difficult to observe that, it is critical to sustain this environment through good schools, recreational centres, correction institutions, skills training centres, career development houses and cultural institutions.

As we seek to build a strong and capable youth, it is not only important for political leadership to lead the creation of a viable environment but also equally important is for the creators of the environment to continuously support it to meet its purpose in the face of changing times and cultures, value systems and technology. This is an important process which should not be glossed over and left to a single institution. A static society is uncompetitive and unsustainable. The society ought to change by modifying its orientation and outlook. It must adapt to changing times and be innovative to reflect her aspirations in order to be responsive to the needs of her youth.

The ability of the society to change and adapt is critical to achieving its long-term goals. The institutions of the society ought to match the fast pace of technology in its infrastructural, mental and virtual contexts.

On the part of *the political elite* in sustaining the environment, it is expected that the elite perform certain key roles. These responsibilities should include:

1. Providing resources for personnel at the National Youth Authority (Commission), for research purposes, stakeholder consultations, public education, training and any other programme designed.

2. Nurturing and growing this environment through revision of policy, performance appraisal of human resource or managers of the Youth Authority, and rewarding performance as the institution achieves set targets.

3. Being prepared to accept change and adjust policy to reflect the same.

4. Holding continuous interactions with the youth and relevant stakeholders to create conducive working relationships among them. These conditions serve as the seedbed for the sharing of their respective strengths and energies needed to implement the goals and objectives of the political leadership.

5. Serving as the primary body for supporting the youth in its endeavours under all conceivable conditions and times.

6. Non-interference in the technical operations of the Youth Authority.

7. Organizing periodic meeting for all stakeholders to deliberate, review and plan for responses to the youth challenges. This should be in consultation with the Youth Authority.

# 3

## Take part in the Political Process but Start Local

*'Politics is almost as exciting as war, and quite as dangerous. In war you can only be killed once, but in politics many times'.*

Sir Winston Leonard Spencer-Churchill (30th November 1874 – 24th January 1965) Two Times British Prime Minister (1940–45 and 1951–55)

Every young person has a role in setting the political agenda. At the launch of *the Springboard (an educational programme) 2010 road show*, Dr Joyce Aryee, a Ghanaian Reverend Minister, made a candid acknowledgment thus; *"While we respect the politicians, we must understand that it is the people who can bring the change for the better through our individual and collective efforts outside of politics"*. The point herein is that, even though political leadership has a role to play in changing the environment, society has the bigger role. With young persons constituting nearly 60% of the population, much rest with them towards the development of the society as well.

This should be seen as a responsibility, rather than a means for agitation. Dr Aryee's point is even more pointed in many African countries where political leaders have become vastly wasteful, corrupt and vindictive to their own citizens. In such environments, the youth or 'we the people' are obliged by a national sense of duty to direct all resources to getting the politicians to serve the people.

There is no doubt that your participation in setting the national political agenda is necessary for ensuring that, the political leadership addresses critical issues confronting you through dialogue. It is not always necessary to confront leadership violently as has been the case on many occasions. Violence and haste do not produce lasting results. They merely create cosmetic benefits, which neither stand the test of time nor genuinely address the concerns you seek.

To this end, your planned and harmonious participation in the political process is necessary. This is important for you to make input into policy. It also helps you to correct the cynical status quo and draw attention to the challenges confronting the youth.

Your participation in addressing the political flaws might not result in short term direct benefits or policy direction. However, ultimately, it can lead to the adoption of viable policies, hence leading to the creation and sustainability of a viable environment. On the other hand, this participation would help you to learn and thus shape your outlook on many issues confronting you.

In seeking to participate in the political process, the youth ought to start from an identified source. Usually it is said 'all politics are local'. That is, you start from your neighbourhood. In school, you could start from the class as class representative, Junior Common Room (JCR) and /or the Student Representative Council level. Those in tertiary institutions could join the student arm of the major political parties on campuses.

Political participation is a practical venture. You cannot participate in the process by reading political literature or sitting on the fence. It is a venture that requires you to make the necessary efforts, take risks and partake in activities of the party or institutions in question. This is where you would begin the actual training of becoming a politician. Indeed the student front and local elections have been established as the foremost areas for your grooming. It provides fertile grounds for learning the tact, rules, and political activism.

It is worth mentioning that, you need not necessarily take part in politics in order for you to have any influence on policy. Through advocacy and grassroots activism, you could mobilise for or against a particular policy. In this way, you could make a substantial impact on policy.

Furthermore, you could, through action groups, mobilize support for campaigning 'a vote against' crusade at elections. This mobilisation could be done through public education, peaceful procession, forums, petitioning, press conferences, online advocacy, newspaper articles and other peaceful means. It is thus worth stating that, these methods are laborious and distant. Nevertheless, they are effective and produce lasting results.

## Take Part in the Political Process

You have an obligation to take part in the political process. This is not to say that, everyone should run for a political office. The thrust of the point is that, you should take part in the discussions affecting you by attending hall meetings, community meetings and activities where binding decisions are likely to be made. As a member of the community, it is important to take keen interest and make your views heard. Your voice matters.

On the operational front, each one of you should take part in processes such as voting, and be prepared to voice your views on related issues affecting your social environment. Take part in the political process. Your single vote means so much. It is a voice. It is an opinion. So do not underestimate it.

Largely, you are mostly affected by the actions or inactions of leadership. You may not win all battles but even in failure, the fact that you participated in the political process should be an enough motivation that, you are part of the political process. Thus you have taken an opportunity to air your views and beliefs.

## The political arena is a slippery ground for any youth

The political arena is a slippery ground for any youth. You are never truly independent. You are usually subject to party's structure and the status quo. It turns some of you into informants, others into bootlickers and still more into bag carriers. Worse still, others lose their purpose in life in the pursuit of recognition and wealth, which the lure of looting-politics promises; this type of politics is not driven by vision and service. This type of politics, characteristic of many nations, does not take pride in building schools, hospitals, or development. Rather, your success in it is marked by how much you've looted for your personal benefit at the expense of the poor, vulnerable and the youth. *Sadly, my barber once remarked to me, "Look at this District Chief Executive; he is very wise. Within four years, he built three houses: one for the mother, a family house and a big mansion in Taifa (a suburb in Accra, Ghana). He says he has three cars: a Toyota pickup truck, a land cruiser and a nice Benz."* The wise loots and the foolish attempts to be honest and come home empty-handed. Once I told my graduate school room mate that, *a Ghanaian politician has stolen an equivalent of $120,000.00.* He retorted, *"Only $120,000.00? In Naija (Nigeria), his family would insult him for stealing such a small amount."* This is how deep the society has sunk. Take up the fight. Your future is at stake.

## Look before You Leap

It does not pay to enter the political fray without purpose or a foundation in life. For this reason, you are advised to gain a foothold in life before entering mainstream politics. That is to say, show maturity in your family life, profession and bring on board skills and appeals needed by the current time and the political tradition you are fraternising with or have joined.

With the many perils in the perpetual battlefield called politics, it is important, first and foremost, to define yourself before entering the profession. You must first set for yourself, beliefs and values, which you are prepared to stand by. These principles should be your guiding light in the course of your grooming and future life. They would serve as guidelines and prevent you from losing your path.

Without personal beliefs, you would miss your sense of purpose and direction. It is important to enlighten yourself and the world about who you are and what you stand for. This is your identity. Thus, when asked what your beliefs are as a politician, you should not hesitate to respond unwaveringly.

Additionally, you should be spiritually matured to stand by essential values such as truthfulness, honesty, fairness, selflessness, and above all, compassion. You must attain high levels of these values if one is not to be enslaved by the lure of power and its trappings.

In 2003, I was in the company of some youth of the New Patriotic Party to listen to the words of knowledge from Dr K.K Apraku, former Member of Parliament and Minister of Trade (Ghana). After a lengthy talk, he stressed and quoted:

*"All politics is local."*

The essence of this quotation, according to him, which of course is attributed to Thomas P. (Tip) O'Neill, Jnr, is that you start your political career from the grassroots. Start from your workplace, home, neighbourhood and community. That is to say that, as you dream of life as a politician, there is the need for you to nurture your dreams from your immediate environment. As you serve your community, the community would in turn propel you to the constituency, regional and national levels.

# 4

## Becoming a Politician: Creating Your Own Armies

*'Mankind will never see an end of trouble until... lovers of wisdom come to hold political power, or the holders of power become lovers of wisdom'.*

*The Foot-Soldier* Plato; The Republic (428/427 BC – 348/347 BC); A Classical Greek Philosopher, Mathematician, Student of Socrates,

Youth leadership structures have come to be important tools in managing youth organisations and harnessing youth potential in politics and commerce for either building, sustaining or moving institutions or society forward. They have also come to be breeding grounds for leadership training and appreciation of the challenges of the same.

Many a national political leader could easily trace their leadership roles to their early days; either as assembly leaders, village organisers, foot soldiers or school prefects or many minor roles in their place of work, neighbourhood, clubs or associations be it professional, social or cultural.

The art of early grooming is indeed important for creating and seasoning you for leadership roles. Moreover, it also helps you to understand the basic machinery of the political system, its dynamics, traps, sacrifices and /or commitments. It helps you at this stage to learn to find your voices and establish your beliefs.

Suffice to say, it is at this early stage that real leaders could either be born or be 'killed'. You pick much of your values at this stage. You learn in part from your role models, and others from other players you come across. At this stage, it is all about learning, growing, taking risks, building networks and bridges and surviving. You are 'the foot-soldier' at this stage.

During this learning period, 'it is not about your academic qualification; rather an instinct for survival and common sense'. You learn to develop an instinct to become part of the political family and attach yourself to the core of the political process.

What you do at the youthful stage in the political arena is never different from any young man starting a career as a banker or an accountant. They pay homage to their bosses, clean their shoes, and do all manner of professional and social errands for them to progress in their career.

The difference between you and your colleagues in other professions is that, you are learning in the beautiful game. It is a game of death; a game where your closest friends could be your worst enemies. A game where there are few to be trusted and most importantly, the name of the trade, which is Politics, is soiled with scandals, looting of national resources and mistrust. The political game is perhaps the only game where internal conflicts on the field of play are fiercer than the attacks from the opposition.

## The Political Profession has a Higher Calling

The political profession has a higher calling and as such, has higher responsibilities. You hold the lives and aspirations of many in your hands. You are critically judged and rightly so, because so many give you so much. You are a leader of men; the representative of your people; the voice, the face and the embodiment of your constituency.

As you enter the profession, remember that, you are being groomed to be a politician. An art you can neither learn from books nor from the plush suites of offices. You learn by participation. You carry posters, plunge yourself in endless debates, stir controversy, stoke fires and do the leg works. Above all when you decide to call yourself a politician, you must know that your solemn duty is to improve the lives of your people. Anything less than this does not qualify you to call yourself a *Politician*.

## *It Is Important to Get a Fall Back Profession*

It should be stated that the beautiful game is not a safe enterprise for people without trade or profession. It should be for those with a profession and value. As a former member of parliament for Lower West Akim, once advised, "Without a fall back profession or trade, I would not advise any young man to enter politics." Thus, to make your path clear, it is important to learn a trade or bring one of the following to the table: money, extreme wisdom and charisma. The safety net is that, no one expects the youth to possess any of these values in adequate measure, hence the need for grooming. What is necessary is that, you should in time acquire skills and knowledge which would make you useful to be an integral part of the political system.

## *Three Routes for Political Development*

For the singular purpose of this book, three progression routes in the field of political profession are discussed.

These are:

1.  Campus Route (e.g: Student Representative Council, Clubs And Churches)

2.  Campus Wings of Political Parties (Grass root Activism and at Home from the mainstream political party)

3.  Traditional route, say, 'Mmerante hene' (Chief of the Youth)

## Campus Route

The campus is one of the most fertile grounds to start your political grooming. It offers opportunities and challenges in equal measure though. By campus, I refer to the Senior High School through to the University, including Teacher Training Colleges, Polytechnics, Nursing, Professional and Vocational Institutions. As noted earlier, you may need to start as class representative to the student representative council, Junior Common Room, house/hall executive which usually include positions as president, vice president, secretary, financial secretary, executive member among others. No position is minor. You can do so much in whatever position you are elected or appointed to, if only you are effective. If you distinguish yourself in a small role, your peers would recommend you for a higher office.

On the other hand, you may offer yourself for election at the school level for an office in the student representative council. There are a number of places for you to start from. It must not necessarily be at the SRC level. You can be elected at Club or Church levels. They are all part of the leadership arena.

National Associations now cut across many campuses. For starters, there is the National Union of Ghana Students, National Union of Polytechnic Students, College of Education Trainees Association, Lions Club, Rotary Club and many more. These organisations also offer opportunities for political growth and development.

## Campus Wings of Political Parties

The second and perhaps the most direct route into the mainstream political profession is through student wings of Political Parties. The major political parties have campus wings on major campuses. In Ghana, the New Patriotic Party has the Tertiary Education Students Confederacy of the NPP (TESCON), the National Democratic Congress has the Tertiary Educational Institutions Networks (TEIN), whilst the Convention People's Party has the Tertiary Students Charter (TESCHART). These arms offer students the opportunity to get into mainstream political activities as well as offer a link to the professionals while on campus.

Moreover, they are grooming grounds for you to learn and have a grasp of politics. Thus many major political parties create the wings on campuses to tap those of you with potentials with the hope that, you would assist in the harnessing of student votes and the rooting of their political ideology on campus. Secondly, political parties use student fronts as grounds for talent fishing for their party machinery and for future leadership roles.

The campus wings of political parties give you direct access to key personalities within your party. It is at this stage that you begin to build the networks, which would later serve a route to your political growth once outside school. It is the 'knowing-the party- base' stage.

It is worth noting that, campus wings become the grounds where political heavy-weights recruit assistants and 'leg men' for their political machine. It is important to observe that, the student wings are not an end in themselves. They are routes to the main political party and as stressed by the Member of

Parliament, for Okere in Ghana, and former General Secretary of the New Patriotic Party, Dan Botwe, "Once you leave school, you must integrate into the party structure to help make the party strong at the constituency, regional and national levels."

The major parties have mainstream youth wings attached to their party structure. The youth wings are well structured from the polling stations through to constituency, regional and national levels. Largely, the youth wings of the major political parties have well-developed programmes which give ample room for youth development in real life politics.

Through youth wings, you witness politics as played by professionals. You learn how policies are formulated, political strategies drawn up and 'warfare' waged. This is neither the backyard politics nor the campus child games. It is the real politics as it is played with its unwritten codes, taboos, conventions and mudslinging. Integrating into the youth wings of the party whilst at school or after school further boosts your acceptance into the political party you have chosen.

## Importance Of Joining The Campus Or Youth Wings

Joining the campus wing of political parties further helps you to polish and affirm your ideological leanings. This is not to make you an ideologue at the expense of reality and common sense. It gives you an identity and commits you to a 'family', which at any point in time would support you in large measure.

The question of identity is critical for future development. Hitherto, identity was a latent concept. It is no longer so. It is now as potent as your beliefs. It defines your circles and networks, closes and opens doors for you, and gives you a base for growth. Political Parties are like a family. Indeed, it is a family where you run for knowledge, warmth and refuge.

## *Start Local*

Upon leaving school or while in school, start politics locally. That is your real base. Your neighbourhood is the real home where you should be known and accepted. Thus, participate in their activities, offer yourself to the services of the ward, zone constituency and the party in whatever capacity. You do all these without asking for a pay-cheque. Your pay-cheque is the trust they would repose in you. This 'trust' is far more valuable than a million-cash.

The beauty of political establishment is that, like the Mother Church, there is a place for everyone: scholars, half literates, illiterates, liars, thieves, drunkards, brawlers, smooth mouths, crooks, informants and gossips. Whatever your skills, the political establishment would have a place for you. It is a field requiring diverse skills in its different endeavours at different times.

It is worth noting that, although unique academic and/ or professional skills are necessary, they might not necessarily be the qualities which would get you accepted in a particular political family. Largely it would be your service, commitment and loyalty.

Therefore, the surest way to get noticed is to serve. Through this, you market yourself whilst telling the base of your party of what you are capable of. It is not about books and much learning alone. If you have ten people with PhD in Economics and similar credentials, whom do you appoint as your Economic Minister?

## Key and Critical Values Required

Values such as humility, willingness to learn, listening, level-headedness, patience and a calm demeanour are essential to your development to the highest levels in any political system. Party elders and groomers look for youth with such qualities and more. Those of you who are prepared to learn and grow up the party or the government ladder would be considered.

Even though the political system has turned many a youth into gossips, informants and fire stokers, sincerely, if you enter the field with the penchant for gossips, that is what the establishment would turn you into: an informant. If you enter the field with a mind for policy, it would turn you into the brains of the realm. The political machinery has a unique way of selection. It selects party leaders, ministerial material, poster boys, loud mouths and all the back room jobs which oil the political machinery.

## You Could Be Leaders of Industry

It is worth stating that, political leadership is not restricted to only party politics. You could be leaders of industry. The Presidents of Association of Industries, Union of Trader Association, and the Trades Union Congress (TUC) and other professional groupings are all political leaders but of a different category from those of political parties. The youth in any industry could aspire to the leadership of any of these professional associations. Like political parties, there could be grooming platform for those of you with political ambitions for their associations. The methodology is quite similar. You learn to network, identify your policy positions on major issues of the association and articulate them in a manner that would be appreciated by the body of your association.

### *The Third Route: The Traditional Setting*

The third option of youth development I would like to comment on is the development of the youth in traditional communities. Traditionally, the Chiefs would train royals to take up royal roles.

Besides these royal administrative roles, there are a number of areas those of you in traditional communities could be trained in. The first and obvious is the 'Mmerante-Hene' (Chief of the Youth). It is a sure route for political development. These positions are equally apt for training and grooming to be better leaders of peers.

In some countries, the concept of assemblymen (council/county members and committees) is also another way of growth by the youth in communities. It offers a route for direct entry into provincial governance. For such offices to be stronger, it is important to urge the youth who gets elected to these offices to make the offices relevant to the needs and aspirations of the people.

It is important to note that, the commentary above is not a blueprint as to what life is in real life politics. The different routes identified here intertwine. You may become the college president and further your aspirations as an assembly member. So it is with political party youth wings. In real life, you normally pursue what is practical and achievable at a point in time.

### *Basic Rules*

Let me state in simple terms some basic rules any youth must observe in the political family:

1.  There is authority in all political parties. The people you see and hear on radio and television might not be the power brokers. There are always advisors, guardians and

handlers around each political party working silently and invisibly behind the scenes.

2. The behind-the-scene powers are largely invisible. They do not wear their power on their sleeves. They are out of the public eye but wield their power through a complex maze of communication channels, tools and resources.

3. There are complex networks within each political party, which is difficult to decipher at the starting block. So be careful to chart the path of honesty, humility and patience

4. Additionally, there could be another network among opposing parties in the political establishment, say between the political parties NPP, NDC and CPP.

5. There are personal interests, which could be so strong to suppress collective party interests. An example is the link between club members, families, and old school associations.

6. It is important to be honest, respectful, hardworking and humble.

7. Look, listen and consult before taking any action.

8. It is absolutely important to learn and acquire a skill, which would make you useful to the establishment.

9. Ferocious burst of anger, stubbornness, strong-headedness and double dealings are sure suicidal vices.

10. It is important to learn the ropes and basic activism if you are to put your vast knowledge base to any good use. There is a man in Ghana called Joe Aggrey, who established himself as an intelligent and knowledgeable sports writer. Upon his appointment as a Deputy

Minister for sports, it was largely held that he would be a Sports 'Messiah'. The sporting community hailed his appointment because it was thought that, he would ignite the sports Ministry with his brilliant ideas. That was not to be. He faded quickly and exited. The game stifled him. Against the machinations and complexities of the beautiful game, his vast knowledge counted for nothing. He had the knowledge but lacked the political skills to survive and achieve his vision. Almost all the successful political leaders you see around started at your age and over the years, learnt and mastered the art.

11. Largely, it is primarily about interests. Policies and principles may be secondary. Thus if you are in a family, say NDC, NPP, PDP or ANC or ZANU-FP and your views do not pacify the centre of power or any other powerbase for that matter, you are likely to be kept at arm's length. A colleague once remarked, "My party is in power, but I am in opposition'. This goes to the heart of the issue. Political 'largesse' often goes to loyalists and 'like-minded pals' than those who are supposedly qualified. I am simply stating the prevailing reality.

12. There are values and rules which each party respects and accepts. Once you opt for a tradition, it is necessary to learn their values, convention and act accordingly. Any careful observer would tell you there is a difference in philosophical approaches to issues by political parties. Note that, knowing these values and rules take time. This call for patience.

13. Be patient as a young man. Cultivate patience. Do not rush to rise. You would come down falling as quickly as you forced yourself upwards.

14. Respect for elders of the party, humility, patience and honesty pay in politics for the youth.

15. Even though a godfather is not the ultimate currency of success, it is important to have one. They are useful, though not ultimate in many instances.

16. If you wish to rise to the top, do not engage in praise singing. With your eyes in your head, be independent minded and truthful to your principles.

17. Do not be awed by personalities. Only bow to superior wisdom. Be humble.

18. Do not go after money or short-term benefits. Keep your senses on the short-term. Plan for the medium term. Project for the long-term goals.

19. Sometimes, your knowledge could be a threat to you. So tread carefully, listen more and talk less. Thus in many situations, remember that, 'sometimes happiness comes from knowing less'.

20. Tread cautiously, seek consensus and put your ideas and views into suggestions.

One evening in 2004 together with friends, about six (6) of us happened to sit at the feet of the then Chief of staff to President Kufuor (Ghana), Mr Kwadwo Mpiani. As the case was in those days, anytime we heard he was in Kumasi, we would visit him, chat, and ask for funding for our programmes on campus. That evening was different.

Unusually, he talked for a long time and gave us 'nothing' at the end of his 'lecture'. We left grumbling. As time wore on, the weight of what he said that evening became apparent and I can say, it is worth more than whatever money he would have given us. At that gathering, some of us were insisting on the apparent 'sins' of the big men in the party and were threatening to confront them publicly on air. Yes, we were hot-blooded with newfound friends in the media who would give us media platform.

Surveying our faces, he started: "The political field you wish to enter is a delicate practice. If you pose yourself as the most knowledgeable, intelligent and all-knowing, you would never succeed. If in your opinion an elder has gone wrong, you do not point it out in public to embarrass him, ... even if he is wrong and you are right, he would not forget the embarrassment."

As he spoke, he ignored us as if he was weighing his words. 'If you do that to embarrass him at this stage in your political life, you are politically weak. He may damage you and you may not recover,' he added. We interjected with murmurs and queries but he ignored us and continued. "If you sincerely believe some party elders are tearing the party down as you say, my advice is that, approach someone whom you think can influence those who are tearing the party apart. By that, you may suggest ways of remedying the errors. If you do that, you would win the trust of the elder you approached as well as solving the perceived problem you are complaining about."

Some of us protested with the view that, it was a long process. Moreover, we would not be recognized as the source of the 'solution'. He equipped, "It pays to be patient and learn. Let the elders take the glory. One day your time of glory would come," he insisted.

He continued: "Your victory in such situations is that, the problem you identified has been solved.... The elder you consulted would recognize your wisdom and discretion. 'He may take your hand or recommend you somewhere unknown to you. It calls for patience, building of bridges and goodwill....''

At that time, it did not mean much to me but as time passed and I came to appreciate the enormity of the beautiful game, I came to respect the man enormously for his summation thus:

1. The foundation for Success is solely dependent on you and you alone. But it takes time.

2. Nothing comes on a silver platter. So use whatever talent and skill you have to survive with dignity.

3. The 'race is neither to the swift nor the battle for the strong' but the one favoured by the base of the party, the Elders and the Public.

4. There are dangers at every step of the way.

## Bid Your Time: Different Traditions and Cultures

Within the much-touted Conservative Tradition, it is a widely held view that, you ought to be groomed before given the opportunity to handle the affairs of men. What is realistic is that, you stay on the sidelines a bit longer, which of course is necessary, considering the huge implications of decisions leaders make. This is a period for you to learn the ropes and acquire the real life experiences needed to adequately handle the affairs of other men. During this period, you are obliged to fraternise with the ranks of the party to prove your worth to the family.

A few months after the New Patriotic Party left office, we paid a visit to H.E Alhaji Aliu Mahama to introduce the Civil Society group, the Alliance for Accountable Governance (AFAG) to him. In the course of our discussion, we raised the issue of the National Democratic Congress government giving room to some youth such as Haruna Iddrisu, Okudzeto Ablakwa, Omane Boamah and Fiifi Kwetey as Ministers and others like John Jinapor, Stan Dogbe, Felix Kwakye, and Fred Agbenyo working in different forms in the government to learn the ropes directly from the front line. In the meeting was a grey-haired man who had been anonymous throughout our conversation. Upon the mention of the youth factor by the Mills' administration, he shot up sharply, "The unfettered youth should not be entrusted with such (Ministerial) leadership."

We all felt a brief silence, but the message sunk in. His utterance was unilateral. The Vice President Aliu Mahama did not seem to give an ear to him nor did he voice support for him but any critical observer would weigh the old man's words carefully. We (AFAG) made our case, but the point was well summed up by the old man.

Within the New Patriotic Party (NPP) conservatives, it seems it takes time for the youth to be given a frontline role. The wrong perception is that, this is by design. In my opinion, it is by accident of time as a result of the nineteen-year rule of the Provisional National Defence Council (PNDC) and the National Democratic Congress (NDC). The eleven years (11) of PNDC rule created a backlog of conservative politicians, who otherwise would have retired by 1992 when constitutional rule was restored.

As naturally as it would be, in 2001 when the New Patriotic Party came to power, these front liners were rightly seen by President Kufuor as the most seasoned hands available and thus kept them at the front lines and the administration of the nation. By this time, their generational compatriots on the other side were fading and /or retiring. So in 2008, when they (NDC) regained power, people like Atto Ahwoi, Totobi Kwakye, Kwame Preprah, Paul Victor Obeng and their generation felt they had no meaningful role at the frontlines. As a result, new faces and relatively young politicians had the opportunity to be at the frontline. Therefore, faces like Rashid Pelpuo, Zita Okine Kwei, Koku Anyidoho, and young faces like Omane Boamah, Agyenim Boateng, Haruna Iddrisu and Okudzeto Ablakwa came to the front line.

There is a fundamental wisdom in the view of the NPP. Thus, given the enormous burden and the weight of decisions political leaders make, it is important for the youth to be associated with power, to learn and gain substantial experience before offering him the opportunity to make direct decisions affecting the lives and aspirations of other men.

There was a deliberate programme by President Kufuor to bring the younger generation into the fold, especially during his second term when he could identify some promising youth.

Youth leaders in the likes of Mohamed Amin Antha, Deputy Minister for Northern Region and later Tamale Municipal Chief Executive (MCE); Razark Abdulai, DCE for Kintampo; Frank Agyekum, Deputy Minister for Information; Emmanuel Asigri, District Chief Executive for Garu Tempane; George Mireku Duker, MCE for Tarkwa Nsuaem; Appiah Kubi Baidoo, Akontombra DCE and many more were given the opportunity to serve their motherland.

One thing is clear among these leaders: besides being leaders in minor roles at a point in time, they had stable and professional lives which had accorded them real life experiences necessary for understanding the turbulence of life so as to pulse them to reflect deeply on the decisions they would later make as leaders.

By observation, the National Democratic Congress (NDC) party seems to hold the view that, the youth must show promise and grow on the job, the New Patriotic Party seems to point out that, the youth must show promise, grow in the shadows satisfactorily before an opportunity would be given to you to continue your growth on the job.

Of these two fundamental views, the former seems popular among the youth. It brings rewards and fruits quicker than the conservatives' position. Nevertheless, considering the enormous tasks of leadership and finesse required for governance, I dare say the conservatives are largely right. This notwithstanding, the youth have proven to be quick learners and have adapted quite naturally to their leadership roles. As a result, they make few errors. Considering the energies and daring overtures and tenacity of the Mills' youth club, it would be difficult to challenge the youth promotion on the basis of preparedness and loyalty.

The fundamental question here is that, if there is another NPP government, would there be new faces as well as young and fresh minds? This would be a turning point in the race for winning the youth. If the old faces resurfaced at the expense of young minds, voices, faces and legs on the battlefields, then there could be no justification for holding the youth back. The NPP will lose the battle for the youth.

Likewise, any political party which refuses to utilise the potentials of the youth is likely to lose the youth race. On a broader scale, any society which refuses to utilise the enormous potential of its youth is likely to be left behind.

Without doubt, many of the youth within the New Patriotic Party have shown promise. Since the party left office in 2009, the legwork, debates and many other activities towards political power have had the youth at the centre or sharing the burden. Many young persons have taken up the burden of working for the party as a full time job without any hope of regular income security.

There is a wider glimmer of hope with the current flag bearer of the New Patriotic Party, Nana Akufo-Addo. By a larger margin, he has managed to blend the youth and the older guards such as Yaw Osafo Marfo, Dr Kofi K. Apraku, Hackman Owusu Agyemang, and Jake Obetseby Lamptey in an effective winning team. Young and energetic youth like Martin Adjei Mensah, Herbert Krapa, Sophia Kokor, Olivia Quartey, Brian Acheampong, Isaac Asiamah, Mike Oquaye Jnr and many others have found their voices, drive, purpose and path in the leadership of the candidate both in administrative and political roles.

## *Two Popular Models Of Youth Development*

There are two popular models of youth development across the continent and many other democracies. There is the model, which makes the youth the spear of the struggle in most political endeavours. The youth wing is made independent, with control over their programmes and activities. And by this they control the direction, pace and mode of their growth without any obvious hand behind the scenes pulling the levers of their power.

This seems to be by far the best model of grooming the youth if all goes well. Nevertheless, it has its serious flaw in giving the youth unfettered power which could be misapplied and could lead to disastrous ends.

As such, it calls for maturity of the youth under this system to guard against self-destruction. It also requires the system to put in place a strong vetting and ideological system to ensure the best is elected and the powers conferred are employed for good. The question of containing or correcting the wayward leadership should be well answered before this system is employed. It is my pick as the best youth development system.

The other model is an *open-yard-system* where the environment is created with the hope that, the worthy would find their way through the door and up the ladder. This system has no deliberate effort or methodologies to groom the youth. It allows the system to naturally conduct the selection process. There is no deliberate poaching and coaching of talents. Those who approach the party are naturally drawn to it by ideology.

In a perfect society, this would have been the best method of attracting talents. But we all know that, other parties are poaching and coaching their next leaders in a deliberate manner. This makes it difficult to trust nature to be kind to the party which believes in natural selection of talents. It is worth noting that, in the real world though, a combination of all the models may be employed.

## Revisiting the National Unions of Students' Bodies

Largely, most National Students' Union bodies have lost their balance to national political parties. Reasons for this are partly mechanical and to an extent convenience. Leadership of national unions is vigorously pursued by political parties for their support and for new blood for their various traditions. Furthermore, student leadership has few options to stay out of the reach of political parties.

In the first place, the cost of winning elections at most levels is expensive; more than the students can bear. For instance, it takes between thirty-five to fifty-five thousand Ghana cedis (GH¢35, 000.00 – GH¢50, 000.00) to get elected as the head of the National Union of Ghana Students. At the campus level, it takes roughly five thousand - seven thousand (GH¢5000- GH¢7000) to get elected to the SRC Presidency. Obviously, these funds are not within the reach of students. This situation coupled with weak fund-raising abilities of candidates, forces students to turn to political parties for funding. With this, student agenda is diluted and to some extent, largely bought.

It is difficult to offer a constructive option out at this stage of our political development, when students on one hand have weak channels for fund-raising. Secondly, major political parties have effective communication channels on campuses, which candidates need for their campaigns if they are to get elected.

Considering the importance of the youth agenda from the students' front, it is important to urge student leadership to claim their independence of thought and freedom. Additionally, it is worth noting that cost of elections could be cut by national associations by considering the culture of raising funds to support candidates who have gone through a vetting successfully. This would, to a large extent, shield them from falling into the hands of political parties to lose their policy platform.

The honest admission here is that, student elections have become extremely expensive far more than the candidates could bear. Campaigning for elections incurs cost in areas such as:

1. Travelling to campuses across the country

2. Setting up and resourcing campus teams on various campuses

3. Media work

4. Operational cost

5. Contingencies

If a national union has about forty affiliates, it would not be difficult to imagine the cost of travelling across the country normally with about two friends accompanying the candidate on his rounds across the various campuses.

# POLICY ISSUES RELATIVE TO YOUR DREAMS

*"A policy is a temporary creed liable to be changed, but while it holds good it has got to be pursued with apostolic zeal."*

Mohandas Karamchand Gandhi born 2nd October, 1869 – 30th January, 1948, was the preeminent political and ideological leader of India during the Indian Independence Movement. A pioneer of Satyagraha, or Resistance to tyranny through Mass Civil Disobedience - a philosophy firmly founded upon Ahimsa, or Total Nonviolent-Gandhi led India to independence and inspired movements for Civil Rights and freedom across the world

## Perspectives

Policies give the framework for programmes and consequently create the prosperous society you yearn for. Once you come to appreciate the policies, it then behoves you to urge politicians to implement some of these policies or similar ideas necessary for creating opportunities for you. They should allow light to shine in their hearts.

Despite the assumption that you and other stakeholders in development would honour your part in the building of a society of abundant opportunities, it is worth noting that the role of policy in setting the baselines and guiding the process is irreplaceable. You would require policy, among others, to define the framework for programmes envisioned for you.

The breadth and depth of the programmes, institutions to run them and manage the policy should be in place as the policy document or reality shall define.

Furthermore, their degree of authority and funding options should also be clarified.

It is important for you to note that, the provision of policy direction by the government is a fundamental requirement for every society intending to create an environment, which would accord every one of you an equal opportunity to become what you want to be.

In the pursuit of this dream, policies should be broad-based to allow for as many required programmes as possible to be created. These policies should be specific to give you an unambiguous direction and above all flexible enough to allow for modification with respect to changing national and youth aspirations.

Furthermore, a national youth policy should have a life span within which certain key targets should be met. For instance, if the policy is geared towards ICT or agriculture, within, say, three to five years, targets set are to be met within this time span. At the end of which the policy would be reviewed and new targets and directions set.

For youth policies to succeed, it should create room for active participation of all stakeholders. There should neither be a condition for participation nor adverse political colouration to the implementation of the policy. The success of the policy starts from the first step. It is never at the implementation stage. Either way, it would be a challenging task to salvage a policy narrowly drafted and seriously perceived as a political tool to suit a particular political ideology.

The European Union's policy framework for your counterparts acknowledges issues of openness, participation, accountability, effectiveness and coherence as critical for governments in pursuit of an effective youth policy. By openness, the consideration is in 'providing information and active communication for you in your language, so that you understand the workings' of the nation including your dreams, ideals, challenges, roles and responsibilities. This should be geared towards availing information to you at any time within the remit of reality and national aspirations.

Furthermore, in 2006 in Brussels, the EU adopted a new strategy for youth policy for the coming decade under the theme: "Youth – Investing and Empowering." Even though it is in respect of the European peculiar situation, it sheds a faint light on our situation. Furthermore, it shows the conceptual basis of policies to reflect on and address challenges within our various societies. This new strategy acknowledges the following facts:

1.  You are one of the most vulnerable groups in society, especially in the current economic and financial inequalities.

2.  You are precious resources. Any new strategy should be cross-sector, with both short and long-term actions, which involve key policy areas that affect you, particularly your education, employment, creativity and entrepreneurship, social inclusion, health and sport, civic participation, and volunteering.

3.  Any new strategy should also emphasise the importance of youth work and define reinforced measures for a better implementation of youth policies.

4. Global engagement is another key consideration. Environmental differences inform policy and thus, policies should address your needs in your peculiar needs and requirements.

## *Ask for Quality Information and Participation*

As much as the provision of free, useful and quality information helps you to understand the society, it also helps to imbue in you the culture of openness as a means of ensuring your participation as a citizen in nation building. It is a learning process and stipulates a culture of respect, inclusiveness and accommodation.

On the other hand, participation, as noted, positions you by 'ensuring that (you) are consulted and more involved in the decisions which concern (you) and, in general, the life of (your) communities.' Your participation in the decision-making process, consulting you on issues bothering you directly and/or indirectly is part of the grooming process.

Furthermore, your involvement helps policy makers tap into your dynamism and skills base. Involving you in the policy process and implementation helps you to identify yourselves as co-owners of the policy and the resulting programmes. It is critical to urge policy makers to acknowledge the tremendous role you could play in policy formulation and implementation. That is to say, your acceptance, ownership, and direct efforts to push through the policy would enhance the success levels of the policy. After all, they are policies to create opportunities for you.

## Demand Accountability From Programme Managers

It is necessary for youth leaders to request that, leadership and managers of youth programmes avail themselves to the scrutiny measured against high management standards as would be demanded from the Chief Executives of public listed Corporations, and thus, assess their capacity to manage the programmes and measure their success levels based on predetermined benchmarks.

The need for feedback is as important as the need for accountability of stewardship. This is important in creating confidence in the institution as well as cementing the bond between you and leadership.

Accountability and feedback ensure a smooth review of programmes at critical stages along its life cycle. Such actions create room for improvement in the programmes and reports of the challenges along the chain of implementation.

Suffice to say, it must be mentioned that, there is the need to design a new mechanism for accountability of stewardship. It is worth noting that, whatever mechanism for accountability put in place should address your reasonable curiosities, aspirations and perceptions.

It should also be mentioned that, whatever policy so designed should also make 'the most of what you have to offer so that (you) can respond to the challenges of society, contribute to the success of the various policies which concern (you) and build the (Ghana, Nigeria, Egypt, Somalia or D. R. Congo and Africa) of the future'. Always remember that, this is a journey every youth aspiring for a prosperous Africa, must be prepared to make.

## *Policies Need Coherence To Succeed*

There should be a sense of unity, commonality and oneness at the various levels of programme implementation. Additionally, there should be 'coherence in developing an overview of the various policies which concern (you) and the different levels at which intervention is useful'. In this manner, the policy would enjoy broad-based support as well as harness your large resource base. If policy makers make the effort to get stakeholders to work together, there is no reason for whatever policies so conceived to fail. Common ownership is a concept that should be pursued by policy makers and Civil Society Organisations (CSOs).

In helping to create a favourable society for you, key areas such as education (including counselling services), employment; training centres, after college skill-bridging training with industry, social service centres and public library facilities should be vigorously pursued.

# 5

## Towards Progressive National Youth Policies

*'Policy aspirations must... be supported in practical (and) material terms if they are to be meaningful'*

National Youth Policy, Malta

It is important to observe that, the dynamics of time, the speed of change and urgency of development call for thei implementation of an elaborate and progressive youth policies and programmes to give life to the policies across Africa. Political leaders and other stakeholders as well as youth leaders should engage each other in creating a national youth policy which would reflect your ideals and national aspirations.

In much the same spirit, petition that political capital and adequate resources should be extended towards implementing the policy as would be necessary to achieve set objectives for creating a workable environment for you. Thus, remind the society, political and traditional leaders that, these objectives are ultimately in your immediate and future interests.

Do not trust in promises. Do not trust many of the political leaders. Many of them are no better than the forefathers who exchanged whole human beings for bottles of wine. Some of these modern ones are worse. They are selling your future for boxes of cigar, photo opportunities and titles. The actions you take today to request responsibility and accountability from them would go a long way to determine your future.

Time is running out for many of our nations to not only draft effective national youth policies but to implement them in a meaningful and practical manner.

It is important for the philosophical underpinnings of the policy objectives to be clearly conceived, defined and supported in the spirit and the letter of the policy. It is within this framework that the nation could achieve the objectives of smart policies necessary to meet the urgent demands of developing your generation by equipping you with skills in solving complex problems. In achieving this, the society would enhance your ability to compete nationally, internationally and globally.

The call for philosophical bedrock for policies is critical, if the society intends to build you for the needs and reasons which best serve our specific national interests. Furthermore, the nation should build the youth not for academic and rhetorical excellence but to imbue in you the moral and spiritual values which create good citizens and serve as the foundation of great societies.

A sound philosophical base is critical so that, say, as you acquire the skills and knowledge to achieve something, you would be motivated to use that skill to serve the interests and needs of the larger society. Thus, whatever the dividends therefrom, would also be at the disposal of the nation. The beauty is that, once you imbue selfless and communal values within your outlook, they permeate your thinking and activities thereby giving you a solid moral and attitudinal foundation needed to make you a better citizen.

## The Central Aim Of A National Youth Policy

The aim of political leadership should not be only about policy and its management, but also other critical areas such as programme design and management of the same need to be considered to meet the actions required by policy. It is important to devote as much energy to programme management as would be accorded to the design of the policy.

Furthermore, the deliveries of the actions to realise the policies are also important. Additionally, 'principal issues, specific objectives and the actions proposed to be taken by various actors' to achieve those objectives should also be clearly defined.

A national youth policy should be well informed on key youth issues such as personal development, skills acquisition, societal values for the preservation of national values, concept and the need for social and national cohesion and integration, hard work, nationhood, entrepreneurial attitude, pride and dignity and personal responsibility. It is important for the policy to give guidance, mould and point out your nation's dreams to you. Additionally, a viable youth policy must lend itself to change in response to emerging social, economic and technological trends without distorting its core objectives.

### *You Need to Embrace the Ideals of Peace and Mutual Respect*

You need to be imbued with 'the ideals of peace, mutual respect and understanding between peoples'. That is to say, you ought to embrace peace as a value needed to stabilize your nation, create an environment of congeniality and continuity and offer opportunities for your growth. Furthermore, respect for each other's views, sense of purpose and shared dreams are inherent in cementing the society not on each other's terms but on common terms which take into consideration your general wellbeing as young persons. This creates an environment of trust and suppresses suspicion and vices, which easily create tensions and tear societies apart.

By interacting among yourselves, even though you are from various ethnicities, you cement the view that you are one people on a common journey with interconnected interests. Effectively, you inculcate in yourselves the thought that achieving one's interests, to a large extent, rests on the goodwill and support of other members of the society. Thus, it is only by working together that you can achieve your individual and collective goals. As a guide, take it that victory is not measured by achieving one person's goals but the collective goals of the society.

## Remember Rural Colleagues and the Physically Challenged

Often, 'subgroups such as young people with disabilities, rural youth and...young women' are left out of the preparation and/ or implementation of policies. The wisdom is that, not only should policies be friendly to them, but also they should be at the centre of policy design and implementation. Their disabilities, weaknesses and flaws neither make them less qualified nor insignificant. Their peculiar nature makes it necessary for them to be involved in the youth development agenda. Understanding the needs of this category of youth, which needs the society most, is critical in achieving a high success rate of any youth policy.

## The African Leader's Pride

The life and breath of African leaders should be to create a society within which the youth could strive to achieve their dreams and (or) the ideals of the nation through thorough policies and realistic programmes. That is to say, the necessary efforts and resources ought to be channelled to these efforts explicitly to bring about the attainment of desired aims of youth policies. That is, there is the need for personal development, social cohesion, integration and development of effective and a confident youth who would be able to compete in this century, be useful to the society and meet the challenges of the times. Such policies should address the facets of problems confronting the youth in their current and future anticipated forms. By achieving this modest objective, the African leader can then take pride in the fact that, he has achieved something for the youth. Anything short of this is a failure.

# 6

## Challenges within Our Societies

*'Most of the problems facing today's youth are not restricted to any single ethnic or religious group, but affect young people generally. Most discussions on youth have focussed on issues such as drug abuse, crime, violence, sexuality and poverty.'*

Unknown

## *Issues to Note When In Public Life*

There is no doubt that some of you are active in the political life of your nations at various levels. Your appetite to help in governance (local to national) is strong and genuine. The above notwithstanding, some of your frustration with the political and cultural systems in place could be sensed and heard on campuses and neighbourhoods. The system you have come to meet is slow to change, devoid of consistent vision and increasingly, many attempts for reforms have been unsuccessful.

Additionally, it has become expensive to get involved in public service. The costs of campaigning and electioneering process have become cumbersome, time-consuming and expensive. This puts enormous pressure on political leadership. Coupled with a high financial dependency ratio of political leaders by society and family members, it is extremely difficult to be in political leadership and survive without being a double tongue or corrupt. It has almost become impossible to be a politician and be descent at the same time. This is not to discourage you from leadership positions but to caution and give you a glimpse of political life as it is to be known in reality to you.

One of the ways of keeping the hands of your political leadership from national purse is for the society to abstain from making financial demands on them. A story is told of one Member of Parliament who locked himself up in his bedroom in order to avoid queues of constituents who had called on him from 5 o'clock in the morning looking for school fees, marriage dowries and related needs. It is said that one man was there for money to marry a third wife!

The call here is for you to appreciate the political environment which is rarely understood by the outside crowd, the pundits, political researchers, free-talking journalists and purists.

## *Your Generation Is Different*

Agreeing with the European Union, your 'sociological, economic and cultural aspects... have changed significantly as a result of demographic changes, changes in the social environment, individual and collective behaviour, family relationships and labour market conditions'. There is no question that, the youth of today is of a different breed from those a decade past.

First, your generation is maturing faster. Under pressure from economic factors (employability, unemployment, etc.) and socio-cultural factors, you are 'on average, more matured when (you) reach the various stages of life: end of formal education, start of employment, starting a family' among others. That is to observe that, you are forced to learn faster and carry larger burdens, which a decade past, you would not normally be called upon to handle. As a result, you grow beyond your years and lose much of the glow of youth to the harsh realities of the environment.

A second point concerns non-linear paths through life for many of you. Today our various life-roles are becoming confusing. It is possible to simultaneously be a student, have family responsibilities, and a job. Many of you are increasingly often torn between these different roles. The 'paths through life are becoming less linear as societies no longer offer the same guarantees (job security, social security benefits, etc.).' It is no longer guaranteed that you would start schooling and complete in one stretch without breaking to take up employment and continue later.

So it is with getting a job right after school. More likely, some of you spend nearly two years on job hunting. At other times, some of you would be pushed by circumstances to start with below-the-line jobs before getting one which best fits your skill level.

# 7

## Specific Policies You Should Point Out to Politicians

*'The greatest tragedy...is not the destruction of our natural resources, though that tragedy is great. The truly great tragedy is the destruction of our human resources by our failure to fully utilize our abilities, which means that most men and women go to their grave with their music still in them.'*

Oliver Wendell Holmes Senior (August 29th, 1809 – October 7th, 1894) A Physician, Poet, Writer, Humorist and Professor at Harvard

## Comments

The dynamics and the speed of the change, the magnitude and the fundamental shakeups they have unleashed call for bold, realistic and holistic policies to address the challenges facing the youth. These changes, which are largely as a result of easy cross border of values, low cost of information, and the diverse availability of the same to you, have torn the society wide opened. As a result, we are witnessing the weakening of the influences of traditional stakeholders such as parents and family in your affairs.

A critical observation is that, the modifications to the fundamentals of our values, society and culture have not matched the speed and sort of changes the floods of information have ushered in. The mode of communicating those values have not also changed much either. Should there be a website where our values and folklore could be accessed or should we still gather by the fireside?

Our educational system, cultural institutions and society have not matched the speed of these changes brought about by globalisation of knowledge, culture, and information either. Among the consequences is that, the foundation of our society is under threat. The identity of the society, its energy to absolve us from pettiness and its ability to build and sustain you has been largely undermined. It is important that government and relevant stakeholders take the necessary action to address issues of progressiveness pertaining to your grooming to overcome these challenges and meet national aspirations.

My aim is to urge you to use advocacy and political positioning to negotiate policies, which would ensure that your aspirations are made centrally in national planning. I should also add that, you would need civil society along the way.

In the following chapters, I attempt to identify some specific policy areas you should urge leadership to concentrate on to ensure that, you are given the necessary opportunities, resources, and support needed to ensure your total development to secure your participation and contribution to solving national and global challenges.

The aims of these policy areas are manifold, namely;

1.  Your development as individuals and groups is so that, you acquire the essential skills and competencies need-ed to meet the current and future developmental goal and challenges.

2.  To help you to gain the attitudes and orientations which would make you key players in decision making and real participants in nation building.

3.  To create and sustain the rich environment which would serve as a platform for your development for you to create, grow and channel your energies into fruitful ventures so desired by the nation.

## *Purpose Of Priority Areas*

Priority areas such as education, job creation, investments, and security among others should tend to serve as the road map for creating the specific needed human values and physical environment regarded as the standard for national youth development. There is no doubt that, this is a fruitful venture requiring national commitment, efforts and leadership.

Efforts should be devoted to outlining specific policy areas, plan of action for their attainment and the challenges stakeholders are likely to confront through a consultative process. Policy areas should be broad, and deeply considered to be necessary as an effective road map. Over the past decade, many governments across Africa and regional bodies have sought to answer the youth question in the face of huge challenges from globalizations, conflicts, constant demographic changes, migration, inequalities in economic gains, unemployment and individualism on your part.

The policy proposals herein, although restricted on their individual merit in answering your questions, their ultimate strength and need lie in their collective strengths where they are seen as one body. Their strengths are mutually reinforcing as well as collaborative. For example, the essence of education cannot be adequately appreciated if it is not considered in the light of skills acquisition for employment, understanding the need to avoid conflict for the purposes of development and social cohesion among other relativities inherent in the chain of activities naturally linked to education.

A plan of action is indeed needed to help government, institutions and stakeholders to implement the policies so chosen. It should, among other things, be relevant to the time and environment. Even though that plan of action may not be holistic and all-embracing, as with earlier works, it should offer a framework for action, direction and support. It is envisaged that, with commitment and push, you can support implementing authorities to implement policies that are as candid and as close as developed and envisaged on paper in its spirit and intent.

With many of our countries having porous and near collapse social institutions for you, it is not far to envisage challenges the government, You and other stakeholders are bound to face in pursuit of such programmes.

## The Nation's Debt To You

The sustainability of an effective and progressive youth policy is challenging but not impossible. This could be achieved 'through joint agreements across all political parties and NGO partners'. This is not to exclude other stakeholders such as the Church and Student Groups.

As a nation, we owe our youth an offer of assistance and support as we would for any other member of the society. We need to ensure that they receive the necessary empowerment, facilities and affection.

Those who are mentally and physically challenged should also receive adequate help to restore them to levels which would make them useful to society. This is our humble debt to our youth, as you prepare to compete with the Chinese, Japanese, the Korean and the Malaysian.

In your discourses and advocacy, do not forget to remind the society of this debt.

# 8

## Education Seen As Investing In You

*'Education is a basic human right and helps one realize his or her human potential. It forms the knowledge and competencies that allow one to thrive at home, in the work place and throughout one's lifetime'.*

Guide to the Implementation of World Programme of Action for the Youth, United Nations, 2006

It is worth noting that, 'the right to education is one that all... youth, including those caught in natural and human-made emergencies, must be able to access'. Many governments are spending on education now. Available United Nations data paints a somewhat encouraging picture: Lesotho spends 10.4% of GPD on education, Kenya, 6.6%; Namibia, 8.07%; Tunisia, 6.4%; South Africa, 5.9%; Cote D'Ivoire, 4.6%; Ghana, 5.5%; Equatorial Guinea, 0.6%, the least on the continent. It is commendable to notice the resources invested in education. These do not of course take into consideration the issues of how funds are distributed across the various sectors of the educational system, nor infrastructural allocations and waste in the system.

It is important to note that, the 21st century is highly skill driven, and as such African governments should be spending an average of 8%, instead of the current 5.8% average. Education has become a dominant variable in an interconnected and skill based world. Even basic commonplace gadgets such as radio sets and refrigerators have become specialized and require a bit of literacy and education to handle.

Government must make sure to make education more skill based and specialised towards selected high employment based areas. It behoves African leaders to break off from the literacy and "classicals" based education of the 1950's and project into the information technology driven education of the 21st century. Governments would have to make conscious and deliberate efforts to make skills based youth education a top priority.

Education as used here refers to skills training, technical education and information technology. Additionally, the balance between humanities and science education should be checked and tuned to emerging high-employing professions.

## Tertiary Education Landscape in Africa

Based upon elaborate source, Africa has about six-hundred and four (604) tertiary institutions. With 6.8% of our tertiary age youth enrolled in tertiary education, there is no doubt that, higher education in sub-Saharan Africa is among the lowest in the world. Regrettably though, the picture is not better on the global stage; 'almost ¾ of tertiary age youth...are not enrolled in tertiary education'. This notwithstanding, with the enormous increment in basic and secondary school enrolment, there is no doubt that many young persons would be climbing up the ladders for advancement in skills and knowledge to improve their employability as they pursue their education. The bright spot is that, in sub-Saharan Africa, according to Shahid Yusuf, William Saint, and Kaoru Nabeshima, 'enrolments' more than tripled between 1991 and 2005, expanding at one of the highest regional growth rates in the world (8.7 %)'.

Despite the fact that tertiary education does not hold the magic wand for development, there is a strong correlation between Gross National Income (GNI) and university enrolment. Without question, it should be understood that normally, 'without substantial numbers of university-trained professionals a country cannot advance'.

There is, therefore, no doubt that 'knowledge has become a key driver of growth and development'. The World Bank further concludes that, 'Countries with higher skill levels are better equipped to face new challenges and master technological discoveries.' Therefore, nations ought to move beyond basic education and concentrate more equally on tertiary education, where 'skills for the knowledge economy are built'. Agreeably, 'improving tertiary education systems should be high on Sub-Saharan Africa's development agenda'.

World Bank lending and credits for education in developing countries has reached 46 billion USD to date. According the Bank's figures, 'for the past five years, annual credits have reached 2 billion USD. From 2000 to 2009, about 21% (USD720) of lending has come to Africa.

In making tertiary education more realistic and meaningful to the needs of Africa's development, priority areas should include:

1. Improving sustainable financing policies amid expanding enrolments;

2. Diversifying tertiary education through technical and vocational training programs, increasing public private partnerships, and encouraging private tertiary education;

3. Strengthening the policy environment and sector governance and institutional management capacity;

4. Improving quality by increasing qualified academic staff and improving quality assurance mechanisms and absorption capacity for new technologies, including ICT;

5. Strengthening labour market linkages through fostering linkages with industry, renewed curricula, and better student orientation; and

6. Enhancing region-wide capacities through regional centres of excellence and knowledge networks'.

*(The above 6 priority areas are adopted online from: Accelerating Catch-Up Tertiary Education for Growth in Sub-Saharan Africa, Synopsis by Shahid Yusuf, William Saint, and Kaoru Nabeshima)*

## Case Study: The case of Ghana at a Glance

The youth of today are in a better position to attain the better education needed for development than earlier generations had, even a decade ago. On one hand, the number of educational institutions of higher learning have increased, even though it is expensive; on the other hand, their course offering and spread are a bit diverse.

According to 2008 data from the Ghana Education Service, there are six (6) public universities and ten (10) polytechnics, and thirty- eight (38) teacher training diploma institutions.

There are eight (8) professional institutions accorded with university status. Three Chartered Private Universities: Valley View University, Oyibi, Dodowa; BookDR University, Nandom; Central University, Mataheko, Accra. University of Ghana has ten (10) affiliate Private Universities. Kwame Nkrumah University of Science & Technology has eight (8) affiliate Private Universities whilst University of Cape Coast has nine (9). Overall, according to the National Accreditation Board (NAB), there are forty-five accredited private tertiary institutions offering degree programmes. It is understandable that, these large number of tertiary institutions offer many course areas of education to many a youth. The point is that, there are larger numbers of university options in terms of programmes for the current youth than there were a decade ago.

A cursory look at the programme offerings of these institutions show a wide array of course options for the youth. These range from the arts through to the sciences to web design and its applications. On the other hand, the cost of education keeps rising at a rate unmatched by economic development. Despite this financial burden, many a youth has shown the urge, drive and ambition to acquire higher knowledge.

University of Ghana has a student enrolment of about twenty-nine thousand, seven hundred and fifty-four (29,754). Overall enrolment at the tertiary level stands over fifty thousand (50,000). This is not to conclude that, there is an oversupply of tertiary schools. According to Prof. Victor Patrick Gadzekpo the President of the Central University College (CUC), Ghana needs a minimum of 50 universities, each with an average student population of about twenty-thousand (20,000) to be able to cope with the soaring enrolment at the lower levels of education.

## The Design of Teaching in Many Countries

As the situation is, from the basic level, teaching lessons seem to be designed for attaining the needed knowledge level, with average emphasis on orientation in our culture and national outlook. Education should not only be a matter of obtaining a Bachelor's degree, Science or any other qualification. It should be a matter of obtaining the right skills and attitudes required by industry, for self-employment and self-sustainability. It should allow for independent thinking and the acquisition of right attitudes which would guide them in the utilization of the acquired knowledge in a responsible manner. Education should lead to self-confidence, realization of one's self, pride and dignity.

At the basic level it is didactic. It does not inspire; it places much emphasis on knowledge and passing an examination rather than laying the foundation for character formation for life in a competitive world.

## *In Focus: Ghana's 1987 Educational Reforms: Brief Lessons*

The 1987 Educational Reforms, which was promulgated to, among others, 'provide broad-ranging manpower supply for various sectors of the economy' through areas such as pre-vocational, pre-technical skills for industry, did not do much to create the required practical skills. The reasons for this shortfall are varied but one is sure to note that, the programme was hurriedly rushed through and secondly, the nation was not prepared for such a drastic change.

It was supposed to help the youth acquire practical skills with self-employability at each terminal point but in the end, it failed in its implementation. First, workshops for skills training were non-existent. Secondly, technical teachers were inadequate to cover the large number of schools spread across the country. Thirdly, there was a large number of course areas to allow for adequate preparation within the limited time span for practical skills.

Fourthly, it should be noted that, the society is still held in the old mentality of children becoming medical doctors and lawyers. This mentality reduced the well-conceived programme to the platform of academic programme. Most parents urged their children to go to school to become engineers and corporate managers and not as masons, carpenters and craftsmen.

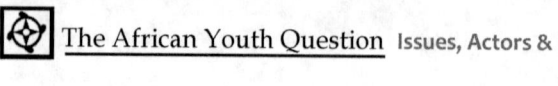 

As a result of these conceptions, students took pre-technical skills (at the basic level), in construction, woodwork, auto-mechanic, electrical and graphic design (senior high school), as an academic programme rather than a skill-based course for direct entry into the job market as the programme document stipulated.

## A Fundamental Weakness

There is a fundamental weakness in many educational systems by virtue of placement of emphasis. Whereas emphasis has largely been on the arts to the neglect of technical education, it is important to observe that, the arts have not been in tune with all areas of national developmental goals which is supposed to include, (Education and Skills Training, Science, Research and Technology, Information and Communication Technology (ICT), Youth and Employment, Entrepreneurial Development, Youth in Modern Agriculture). The picture is that, there is not much continuous effort on the side of policy direction to ensure that our educational system points to our national youth development plan. For instance, we talk about ICT as the new gold mine, but realistically not much has been done to train many of you by way of institutional education. Nor much infrastructure widely built to support this thinking.

In Ghana, ICT education is a key part of the new National Youth Policy; but of the nearly fifty tertiary institutions, it is about only three Private Universities (Ashesi, All Nations University College, and Presbyterian University College) out of the fifteen (15) surveyed, which are training ICT students at the level employable by industry. On the other hand, with the public universities, Kwame Nkrumah University of Science

Technology offers programmes in computer science. The University of Ghana has an elaborate programme to create hotspots and ICT facilities to give any student an opportunity for self-tuition or access to the World Wide Web. This venture is commendable. The university has rightly concluded that, access is a prerequisite to making information available to their students.

This initiative though, is not the high level ICT platform being advocated to create elite programmers. Nevertheless, it surely gives access to the world-wide web and information for self-tuition though.

It should be understood that the availability of hotspots and computers would not necessarily be of much use if you are unwilling or unable to utilize the facilities as tools of learning. Suffice to say, it is important to acknowledge further that, one does not need a formal university degree in ICT to become career oriented in the field. It is possible to enrol for an ICT professional programme whilst pursuing your original academic course.

By accident of expansion, private internationally recognized ICT trainers like NIIT, Intercom Programming and Manufacturing Company Limited (IPMC) and Advanced Institute of Technology (AITI) have established centres in Ghana and in many African nations. These institutions offer quality realistic routes for many young people desiring for a career in ICT.

This is welcome news, but the cost of tuition is an issue that could be considered for an intervention by public or private fund to subsidise the cost. In return, the funding institutions could ask for a share of salaries and future programmes that would be written by beneficiaries.

*Request For An Elaborate Technical Skills Education Programme*

There is a strong opinion in development circles to allow, deliberately, technical education to take precedent over arts and language. Technical education, also including engineering, ICT, and electronics, creates enormous job opportunities; it employs lawyers, accountants, secretaries, and front office managers.

Furthermore, the creation of one engineer, software developer, and a furniture 'master' could create thousands of jobs along the chain of production to delivery to consumers when you consider downstream and upstream interconnections. It is hard to see how a 'lawyer' could create such massive direct job opportunities.

One software engineer or a carpenter could create jobs on the upward for lawyers, managers, accountants, marketing personnel, drivers, cleaners, security experts, and advertising agents among others. On the downward, they support the supplier of raw materials which are needed to support the manufacturing.

In simple and frank language, these technical creators feed and keep the service sector afloat. Advertising agency for example, would not exist if there are no manufactured products or ancillary sectors. Yet most systems create more arts graduates than software developers, engineers, furniture workers or artisans and entrepreneurs.

The argument here is neither to denounce the arts nor demean their immense contributions to national development. The emphasis here is that, the priorities seem biased towards the arts even though they barely create large scale direct and auxiliary jobs. More and more, it seems technical education is looked upon with disdain and students enrolling in technical institutions are considered with a dint of failure. Those holding this view are narrow in their considerations. Technical education has a central role in the development of any nation even if it is largely at the middle levels of industry.

There is a cynical view that, this status quo is barely challenged because, most of the political leadership, and policy makers who are tasked to create the needed balance among technical education, the sciences and the arts, are mostly of the 'humanities' stock.

This might not be entirely accurate. That is to say, it is cheap to start and run these humanities courses (board and marker). Thus, you only need a lecture room, a marker a board and a resource person whereas with the technical programmes, machinery, physical infrastructure, maintenance and computers require expensive initial capital expenditure.

Technical education in the country (excluding ICT) should go to the highest level of skills acquisitions in all its areas of training. Thus, the higher levels of education should be defined by higher mental development, higher skills and expertise to design high end products and solve complex technological challenges and not be denoted by certificates.

## There Is the Need For Technical University

On the traditional front, it should be ensured that there is a coordinated and progressive technical education. This could include creating a progression route for technical institutions to the doctorate level with substantial industrial practical workload. To this end, there should be a University of Technology to purely cater for technical education and research work. Or for the purposes of cost and space, an existing university should be restructured to accommodate this need. In this vein, there would be the need to clearly define technical education in the context of national aspirations and peculiarities. In Ghana, for example, the Kumasi Campus of the University of Education, Winneba would suffice. On the other hand, if the current 'invasion' of Kwame Nkrumah University of Science Technology by social sciences and humanities could be reversed, then obviously it could be redesigned to accepting this role.

This Technical University should have high concentrations of practical work load such as masonry, furniture work, ICT and related programmes. The emphasis is on real work after which graduates are expected to fit directly into the job market.

## Roles of Parents, The Mass Media and Traditional Authorities

The lure of education far outweighs its cost, albeit expensive. An educated youth is a far greater asset to a nation than a thousand of them without basic education and or skills to contribute towards national development. With employment stagnation within the humanities in many economies, Civil Society Organisations (CSOs) and the youth need to ensure that, it becomes the preoccupation of policymakers and development practitioners to deliver on the ultimate need of the nation to contribute adequately in developing technical, vocational and skills education as well as diversifying school programmes.

A key note is the fact that, education as stated here is not restricted to structured curricula in educational institutions. It goes beyond to include your acquisition of essential practical skills and attitudes needed to meet the challenges our development needs spring at you.

Furthermore, governments in implementing our educational policy should not only restrict their vision to the ability to read, write and communicate and the attainment of academic knowledge alone. These are inadequate. They should be equally concerned with the attitude, toughness of will, sincerity of purpose and mentality which would lift you from your mental poverty, ignorance, *believe-everything-West* disease and challenge you to employ your minds to create a better society. You need an education which would challenge you to change your minds to believe in your abilities and potentials to create your own wealth, comfort, and security.

The engineers who built the London Bridge are no different from the Ghanaian, or Senegalese engineer. So are the medical doctors and software developers who are making breakthroughs in their respective fields of endeavour. The difference lies in our thoughts, toughness, attitude and horizon. You need a global mentality which would enable you to deploy your expertise to make you competitive in the global marketplace in an era where technology has changed the fundamentals of employment, development, business, commerce and most endeavours.

Demand your right to be equipped with the tools you need to meet and overcome the challenges this century poses. If by going through an educational system you come out without the adequate skills to meet challenges and 'solve complex problems', then it is your duty and that of society to question leadership on the viability of the educational system which is in place and why the system has failed.

On a cursory look, there is no question about depth of policy with respect to our intentions about our educational systems. Two challenges emerge here though. These are your focus in life and the infrastructural support to the programmes and the systems as a whole. It seems many of you have misplaced priorities and your attitude to life does not encourage reluctant politicians to commit resources to your development. It is said that, many of you are giving politicians justification for their indifference and failures.

There should be no doubt in your minds, and those of politicians, traditional leaders and policy makers that, certificates as they have come to be, are not enough for your entry into the job market nor survive in it. So in testing the viability of an educational system and making it viable to you, skills, mental attitude to work and on the job performance should be at the heart of consideration.

## The Educational System Should Suit Industry

With the private sector expected to be the engine of employment, it is reasonable that their position should be taken into consideration in policy sessions and reviews. This leads us to accept that, there is the need to identify and respect the skills requirements, competencies and attitudes which you would need to survive the modern work environment. It is questionable to train graduates who industry does not trust as competent and ready for the job market. The educational system should be close to Industry as much as possible to ensure that graduate at the terminal points have the relevant skills or industrial experience required by the job market.

## *Necessary Forms Of Education*

Education can be considered from three main areas, namely cultural education, formal education and non-formal. Cultural education should be on the teaching of our values as a society. These values are critically important for a number of reasons.

Firstly, the values of the society serve for identification purposes. It would not be prudent to develop you in isolation, without you knowing where you are coming from and what defines you and your society.

Secondly, your cultural values further serve as the foundation of the society. These foundations have ultimately served as pillars holding the society together as one people in peace with ourselves and mother earth, the rivers, forest, the animals and natural resources.

For years, they have withstood assaults and wars without total collapse. Your cultural values are walls of defence in the storms of growth and development, which reminds you of our roots. Thirdly, these values are so rich as to impact certain key values such as hard work, dignity, communality, generosity, respect for life and property, love and appreciation of peaceful co-existence and forgiveness which are more than ever relevant in these modern times.

## Cultural Education Is Faltering

Cultural education, which is centred on our rich values and traditions, is taught in most schools. The break point is the disconnection between what you are taught in schools and what we are actually practicing in our daily lives as a society. They are at variance with each other. We educate the youth to avoid corruption, yet we are corrupt. We educate the youth to cherish honesty and fearlessness, yet we are dishonest and cowards. We educate the youth to embrace love and compassion, yet we are full of hatred and bitterness. We teach communality, sharing and contentment, yet we are greedy, selfish and mean. We educate the youth on the benefits of hard work, yet we are lazy. It is absolutely strange that in practice, we are different from what we teach. We educate our youth to cherish excellence, yet most of us are mediocre in our endeavours. Indeed, we even reward mediocrity.

No wonder the youth is losing much of our identity in the midst of nationhood and globalisation of culture, ideology and modernisation.

Africa ought to use cultural education to claim the lost richness back. We cannot educate our youth in absentia nor should we allow only the ability to read and write and acquisition of certificates to become the golden keys. Rather, our efforts should be to train patriotic and well-rounded youth. In the midst of this distorted system, we have had so many university graduates, yet our society has not gone beyond the verge of begging and squalor as a result of corruption, greed, laziness, selfishness and cronyism.

We need to create a modern youth who would appreciate education as a total experience between literacy, numeracy and values. Such would have to appreciate that, the essence of education is to help solve challenges facing the society.

We have courses in our educational syllabi with the hope of inculcating values into our youth. The true situation is that, students read these values to pass examination rather than with the intention of using them in their daily lives.

This goes back to the root of the problem. Central government cannot use formal education to imbue these values in the youth. It would only be a scratch on the surface. We can only imbue these values by our lives, character and attitudes within our homes, communities and workplaces. As such, parents, politicians, traditional and religious leaders ought to set examples for the youth by leading exemplary lives. The emphasis is on private lives and not their public lives, which new and old media technologies portray to the world.

It is up to our traditional leaders to re-emphasize the culture of storytelling, the family unit (close and extended), and the communal system which existed at the birth of our society. Parents should begin to spend time with their young persons. They should educate them and try as well to live moral lives for them to emulate and polish. It is time to take leadership roles in the education of the youth from the mass media.

### Using the Mass Media to Reach the Youth

We could adopt the radio, television and social network portals to educate the youth with the aim of getting them imbued with our values. This should not be the work of formal education, which has so far been effective in producing a large number of literate and certificated youth who turn out to be less useful to industry. The need for using mass educational means such as radio and television has become more necessary against the backdrop of their extensive reach. One uncertain variable though, is the number of youth who listen to the radio, read newspapers and have access to televisions. This uncertainty notwithstanding, the radio could be the starting point.

## Education Is For Better Life

Another dimension regarding your education is your ability to have a clearer understanding of life and to appreciate the direct bearing of your academic knowledge on the life you would eventually lead. That is, the skills to survive and fend for yourselves, thereby translating 'classroom-knowledge' into your lives such that the link between academic learning and real life would be established. Education is supposed to transform your life. It is a tool for personal and national development.

It is important to establish the need for you to consider your education as wholesome not because you passed your final exams. Rather, because you have acquired the attitudes and character to survive in the real world whilst at the same time, serving your expected roles as the eyes, ears and the future of the society by virtue of your acquired knowledge.

## Dropouts and the Academically Weak

For a long time many societies have had the stubborn situation of school dropouts and many have gone through basic level of education without the requisite basic skills. In Sub-Saharan

Africa, school dropout, rate is as high as 42%. According to Global Education Digest; dropout rates are; 'Chad (72%), Uganda (68%), and Angola (68%)'. The situation is better in 'Mauritius (2%) and Botswana (7%).'

Moreover, there are those of you whose interest and academic ability and opportunities would not permit you to pursue a higher level of education. The educational policy should address the needs of these classes. In the case of these classes, informal education should make it possible for these groups to acquire the needed literacy and orientation. It is important to strengthen the informal education centre. The youth needs to survive and make a meaningful contribution to the society, and it is only education which could imbue the necessary skills and resources.

## *The Need for Multiple Assessment System Scheme*

It is worth noting that, standardised common educational system adopted by many societies should be reconsidered to ascertain if it is suited to our environment against the background that, we have serious disparities in infrastructure, social amenities, human resource, and inhibitive cultural practices. Questions could be raised if students at privileged and well resourced institutions, (that is, those with motivated teachers, tools and technical equipment, classrooms, teaching materials and other necessities of learning in schools) should be examined on the same examination standards and along the same school term period as students in challenged areas who have no access to basic requirements for effective learning, classrooms, furniture, teachers and learning materials.

In this direction, it would be necessary to create a step-system within the educational system to cater for students in the challenged communities. That is, under this system, these students could be made to undergo basic or secondary school education a year or two above the stipulated duration. Or students should be encouraged to sit for the exams when they are prepared and ready and not within a mandatory number of years.

This should be a time-limited provision till the communities concerned are resourced with the requisite resources to imbue the pre-requisite knowledge and skills. It is better for students to prepare adequately for examinations and life than to drag them through the educational system for them to fail in life. Such a failure would daunt their confidence and leave a scar of fear and inferiority on their minds.

## Quality and Affordable Higher Education Is Your Right

It is important to observe that, higher education should not be a privilege but a right to every young person because of its need as a prerequisite for national development. It works for a nation's competitiveness and her pursuit for excellence in research and development. It could 'play a key role' in Africa's 'catalytic economic growth'. As Obiageli Ezekwesili, (World Bank Vice President for Africa) observed, 'We have made a lot of progress in primary education, but we can't stop there.' Obiageli continues, "Africa's population is seeing a 'youth bulge', and so we simply cannot avoid tertiary education—it has to be the bedrock of Africa's development." We cannot 'continue business as usual—education must meet the needs of the economy.'

Furthermore, a World Bank educational analyst agrees that, 'Africa urgently needs doctors, nurses, agriculturists, engineers, administrators, lawyers, and business leaders.' Of course, common sense and casual observation would easily concur with this observation.

These are age-old concerns, that more young persons must be trained to acquire education, values and capacities; where higher education should mean higher skills, more competitiveness and being of higher value to industry, yourself and your society. From a simple premise, an MSc Marketing graduate should be better in breadth and depth in academic and personality dimensions to industry and society than a BSc Marketing graduate.

## Parallel District-Based Skills Education

Beyond Basic Education, Districts, Municipalities or Regions should be resourced and authorised to train the youth in the disciplines and skills to meet a local development agenda based upon the competitive advantage of the locality. That is to say, parallel skills training should be allowed to exist alongside national curricula.

In other words, Skills Training and Employment Placement Programmes (STEPs) and National Vocational and Training Institutes (NVTIs) should be collaborative in this venture.

## Young Persons in Conflict Areas

The issues of youth in conflict areas and hotspots need to be considered in order to make sure that, those of you in these communities are not left behind and (or) many hurdles placed in your path. Already in such areas, we have seen how education, business and development have been hampered by the conflict. Schools could be closed for months and often interrupted. Businesses are either closed or burnt down. With a uniform national curriculum and timeline, without specialised systems for these areas, it would be difficult for those of you in conflict areas to follow along.

Likewise, in other areas such as security, homelessness and abuse, painstaking efforts ought to be expended to make sure that those of you in conflict areas have your universal rights respected under your respective sovereign nations within a common time frame of education as any other youth in the country.

In the pursuit of programmes for young persons in conflict areas, a first suggestion is to start from the mind in order to change attitudes and focus your dreams on the future for prosperity, fulfilment and peace. Winning the minds should be foremost. Drama, role-play and dialogue among the youth of the various tribes, interest groups would play key roles.

In these activities, you should be engaged in meaningful progressive dialogue where each side of the equation would be heard through your own acceptable means without restrictions, intimidation and coaching. This should not be a short run programme. The government and key players to be involved in this process should be prepared for a long and turbulent process.

Views of religious groups should be solicited in programmes designed to ensure the continuity of education and youth programmes in these designed activities. This would be a demanding and costly venture. Nevertheless, it is important to take note of the cost of large numbers of you in a conflict area.

Without such assistance, the youth would grow without skills or trade to help in the meaningful development of the society. The modest conclusion that could be made is that, these youth would turn out to be outcast, thugs, delinquents, gangsters and armed robbers. The negative toll of their activities on society and national development should encourage us to avert it now by committing energy and resources to this cause.

One critical constituency in many of these conflict areas is Political Party Politics. Even though, there has not been a widely accepted factual basis to suggest their duplicity in the issue, the wide and common perception is that, many politicians are more of a part of the problem than a partner in solving the problems in conflict areas. As such, their direct involvement at the grassroots level might rather be counterproductive. They should rather play supportive roles to civil society and other groups behind the scenes.

## Employment Categorisation of The Youth

It is essential to identify the current categories of the youth as they exist in our society so as to enact policies and programmes, which would specifically deal with their peculiar needs. Without adequate understanding of their aspirations and concerns, it would be difficult to manage their needs and challenges in a comprehensive manner.

Thus, employment categorisations of the youth include:

1. *Young Entrepreneurs*: They are the educated, skilled or the uneducated among you who are managing their own flourishing businesses. For some youth, these ventures could be their second jobs.

2.  *The Educated and Employed*: these include Senior High School to University graduates. These are the gainfully employed at their skills levels.

3.  *The Educated and Unemployed*: These are those of you without employment after school. You are searching for jobs and attending interviews though.

4.  *The Skilled and Employed*: These involve those in artisanal trades such as seamstress, tailors, carpenter etc.

5.  *The Skilled and Unemployed*: These are those of you who have completed skills training but lack the resources to start your own businesses or find a 'master'.

6.  *The Marginals*:

    a.  *First Category*: These include the skilled youth who are self employed but are barely able to survive as a result of saturation in their respective industry and lack of skills in the business side of their respective trades.

    b.  *Second Tier*: These are the employed educated among you who are paid below the minimum wage.

7.  *Traffic Light Entrepreneurs*

    a.  *First Tier*: These are educated or skilled youth who, failing to secure jobs, have chosen to hawk and sell under traffic lights and market places.

This category normally does so with the purpose of saving money to start their own businesses or furthering their education.

b.  *Second Tier*: These are the uneducated youth who consider hawking as a means of survival. Migration to higher levels of entrepreneurial activity is not a priority but would embrace and change when available. Over time, their accumulated entrepreneurial skills are able to project them to the next level of entrepreneurship.

c.  *Third tier*: These are the youth, uneducated and unskilled youth, who have taken hawking as a life long occupation.

8.  *Workers*: These are the youth who work as farm labourers, house helps and other menial jobs.

9.  *Rural Youth*: These are the masses of you who are resigned to rural communities with or without opportunities at all. They could be ambitious and skilled but their rise is limited to the number and level of opportunities available.

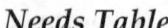 

## Needs Table

| CATEGORY | NEEDS | ACTION |
|---|---|---|
| Young Entrepreneurs | 1. Technical advice on business management<br><br>2. Low interest Loans<br><br>3. Access to market<br><br>4. Favourable business environment<br><br>5. Policies to reduce business constraints | 1. Incubation Centres<br><br>2. Loan guarantees and grants<br><br>3. Establishment of SME Bank<br><br>4. Redirection of the Venture Capital Fund |
| The Educated and Employed<br><br><br>The Educated and Unemployed | Good salaries and conducive working conditions<br><br>1. Jobs<br><br>2. Retraining to increase employability<br><br>3. Entrepreneurial training | Higher minimum wage, tax breaks<br><br>1. Improve business operations<br><br>2. Encouragement of FDI's<br><br>3. Advice to take up part time jobs<br><br>4. Entrepreneurial opportunities |
| The skilled and Employed | 1. Technical advice<br>2. Business training | 1. Link to youth skills training facility |
| The Skilled and Unemployed | 1. Funding<br>2. Office Space<br>3. Entrepreneurial Skills | 1. Link to SME Bank or Venture Capital<br><br>2. Link to a private funding with government guarantees |

| | | |
|---|---|---|
| *The Marginals*<br><br>*a. First Category*<br><br>*b. Second Tier* | 1. Build a large customer base<br><br>2. Increase remuneration<br><br>3. Entrepreneurial and Marketing skills | 1. Pick up a second job<br><br>2. Ask to start a business<br><br>3. Ask to join youth skills training facility |
| Traffic Light entrepreneurs<br><br>*a. First Tier*<br>*b. Second Tier*<br>*c. Third Tier* | 1. Needs funding support<br><br>2. Needs necessary skills and direction to contribute in a meaningful manner to national development | 1. Open to incubation centres<br><br>2. Open to SME bank<br><br>3. Introduction to youth skills training facility and other related programmes. |
| Workers | 1. Education<br>2. Skills<br><br>3. Good working condition | 1. Education<br><br>2. Skills: ICT, entrepreneurship<br><br>3. Introduction to labour laws to ensure they fight for Good working condition |
| Rural Youth | 1. Education<br><br>2. Skills | 1. Introduction to opportunities available to the youth |

## Emerging Education Pattern among the Youth

Shorter growth periods coupled with the sharp change in the youth structure has created many routes to development or better put, the youth have created a number of routes for their personal development. This change has to a large extent made full time scholarship less popular and perhaps encouraged productivity. Ten observations have been made here:

1. The first group is full-time students supported by parents or guardians.

2. There are some of you who are working professionally and schooling at the same time without support from families.

3. The third group are those of you who are in school and have families of your own.

4. The fourth group are those of you in school, who work to support yourselves and your families.

5. The fifth are those without education and as a result are selling on the street.

6. There are those with education and /or skills but without jobs. The unemployed graduate.

7. There are those without education and as such without jobs.

8. The eighth is those growing as house helps, farm hands against their will.

9. The ninth category is those working as apprentice in informal and unregulated sector.

10. And there are those in the 'gutter', without direction or any sense of purpose.

The requirement of these categories of youth varies and policy consideration should reflect their peculiar needs. Despite the growing popularity of these routes, many of you fall behind. It is, therefore, important to help keep the youth in schools and training centres. The National Youth Authorities (NYAs) should take a central role by creating a pool of opportunities to accommodate those who are vulnerable among you.

The idea of temporal foster homes should also be promoted across endemic areas. This would allow you breathing space to pursue education and (or) skills training. The funding of these homes could be left to philanthropist and Community donations. For the sake of your future, urge government to subsidise the cost of running some of the selected temporal homes.

Additionally, it is important for the homes to be regulated. The enforcement of the regulations is as equally important as the regulations establishing them. For this reason, a NYA should be resourced to undertake this role.

### The Issue Of Girls Needs More Attention

This issue of girls has had its share of publicity and complexity. These have over time shaded its essence in the current environment. This notwithstanding, it is important to consider that, this issue is as important a decade ago as it is now. The quota system in some Universities has been a positive welcome to help the question of girls and young women but your graduation and integration into the job market has largely been problematic.

Traditional concepts of job have reduced the range of job options for many females as a result of employers' restricted views based upon the status quo. As the situation is, many jobs have been branded as male jobs and thus it has become a barrier to young women even if they are qualified.

It would be impossible to advocate for job quota system for young women as it has been done in many tertiary institutions. Perhaps at this stage, the young women would have to paddle on their own strengths and merits. This calls for added skills and proactiveness on their part to excel at interviews and other endeavours such as advocacy considering the male dominance on many endeavours of life. A candid observation is that, many of you women when given the support would be very capable to succeed on your own without treating you as weaklings who would cry at any petty issue.

## Rural Young Women Have A Peculiar Case

There is the need to consider the case of rural young women. At a younger age you undergo the burdens of rural life which makes your situation more precarious. Coupled with the challenges of poor educational resources, there should be an urgent commitment to ensure that, special provisions are made available to you by way of lowered entry requirements or a quota system into Secondary and Tertiary Schools.

Performance award schemes could also be considered. Scholarships and counselling services in areas such as course choices, combination of house and farm chores with academic life and career aspirations should also be made available to you unconditionally. Additionally, those of you suffering from extreme cultural practices which your counterparts in the cities have largely avoided should voice it out. These practices, undoubtedly, prohibit your opportunities to develop and pursue your dreams.

As a former village teacher, I have come to observe that, by reason of environment and perception, many of you have lost confidence and initiative. As such you are slow starters. Most of you pick up to become bright students when given the opportunity.

In order to help you to build your confidence, school textbooks ought to reflect 'positive representation of successful African women' in their case studies and examples. These needs would not come to you on a silver platter. You would have to work for them.

## Pregnant Young Women

The stigma of pregnant young women being in school should be considered with the intention of keeping them safely in school without harassment, intimidation or stigmatisation. Even though they got to their present situation largely by their ill-advised actions, what is at stake here is their innate potential to help in national development and further prevent them from becoming a burden on society later on in life. They made a mistake and the society should be there for them. They require a second chance.

Each of these young women, with proper education could turn out to be a female entrepreneur or scientist we admire. They are assets to the nation and we should not allow the temporal setback of early pregnancy to drive them to waste.

Towards bringing them up to the level of usefulness to the society, their medical care, relative to the pregnancy, should be borne by parents or family (if they are capable), community or the state.

The Department Of Social Welfare in association with The Ministry of Education or the appropriate Authority should create a database of these young women some of whose cases could be as a result of rape, environment and circumstances they were largely unprepared for so that support could be given to them specific to their peculiar conditions.

Often the case is that, they are largely left on their own. The popular phrase to them is that, 'If you are ready to play adult games, then you should be prepared to buy your own plates.' The simple point I am advocating is that, no youth should be left behind no matter the cause(s) of their circumstance. Let us pull every youth along as we strive for a society better for all. I believe in reformation. I believe in second chances for the youth. I believe that every youth, when given the right environment, guidance and opportunities, is capable of climbing to the highest stairs of life to achieve his dreams and aspirations.

## To the society: Legal Age of Marriage

Underage marriage and betrothal in certain communities persist at the expense of young women. Poverty, abrasive religious inclinations and inimical cultural practices have all played a part in the poor state of female youth in traditional rural communities. Getting proper education, the right attitude and perspective is critical in building them up for the challenges of real life. It has been suggested that, besides educating mothers on the values of female education and reforming dark spots in our culture, it is important to 'raise the legal age of marriage' to avert, to a large extent, the incidence of under-age marriages among female youth.

It is important to protect them from sexual harassment, subservient roles in the home and ensure their full participation in the full life of the society. The current legal age for marriage which is at eighteen (18) years in most countries is apt. The critical point is to identify these societies in which underage marriages occur and take legal actions against them. Raising the legal age of marriage would not solve the problem entirely.

# 9

# Science and ICT Policy

*"To raise new questions, a new possibility, to regard old problems from a new angle, requires creative imagination and marks real advance in science"*

Albert Einstein (14th March 1879 – 18th April 1955); German Born American Who Developed the Special and General Theories of Relativity. Receipient of Nobel Prize for Physics In 1921

## Comments

Many educational systems have come far in traditional science programmes in Chemistry, Biology and Physics. In Ghana, the government's policy in the early nineties to select one Secondary School per District to use them as Model Schools for Science and ICT development was a good start but obviously sustainability became an issue until 2001. Subsequent provision of internet facilities at Second Cycle institutions also point to the good intentions of politicians and governments. Rwanda, South Africa, Kenya, Egypt and Mauritius and many few other countries are gradually placing ICT at the centre. Suffice to say, in the real world you live, these basic initiatives would only serve as appetisers to motivate you to aspire for the greatness of ICT.

With the enormous pressure to pass paper examinations and gain entry into universities, many of you at the secondary school level largely concentrate more on their examinations than the lure of ICT, besides browsing, checking of Emails and social networking sites. The real effort should be outside the classrooms, where you would be faced with prospects of life and career dreams. Thus you should seek to push for an ICT policy that seek to provide opportunities for you in training and courses capable of providing you with high-end skills.

A realistic effort would be to support you to learn employable skills in ICT such as CISCO's Networking Programmes, Programming, Data Analysis and other modules sought after by industries. Thus, efforts would have to be made in equipping you to be able to sit for professional courses if the government indeed wants you to be employable by industry. These are the sort of issues student leaders should seek to influence.

Governments need an ICT development policy with targets to run not less than a twenty-year period. These policies should train African youth to take frontline roles in ICT endeavours for the continent; first for cyber security; second as IT professionals for our industries, and thirdly as exports to the world. Opportunities for employment in IT are limitless. Africa needs to take advantage of the space. Africa has the capacity to train not less than a quarter of a million ICT specialists annually in the next decade. India experimented with it and succeeded. Almost all major IT firms are in India; IBM©, Microsoft©, Apple©, Google©, CISCO© and many more. You have Indian IT graduates working all over the world, remitting tens of millions to home annually. We need the vision and the commitment to deliberately train a sizable number of our next generations of youth as IT specialists.

## Push For A Technology (ICT) Development Fund

Considering the huge job creation and financial potentials in the ICT industry, it is important for governments to take leadership roles in training middle and high levels ICT professionals for both the local and international markets. In this direction, there should be an annual fund to meet the ICT training needs of the nation for over a period of time, reasonably a twenty-five (25)-year period.

## The Use of the Fund

The fund should go to three (3) tier sectors.

The *1st Tier* is private universities which have existing ICT programmes. This should be for

a.  Faculty development

    b.  Infrastructure development

    c.  Acquisition of equipments in the form of computers, servers ...,

    d.  And Subsidy for school fees.

With the exception of the School Fee subsidy, the rest should come as a long term low interest loan. The term for payment could be between 7-10 year periods. With respect to the fees, a quota system should be used, based on a competitive basis, managed by the Council for Tertiary Education.

The *2nd Tier* deals with private professional ICT education providers which fall outside the traditional mainstream tertiary education such as NIIT, IPMC, and AITI. With this tier, government should invest in the cost of tuition subsidies. Incentives should be given to centres which help students to get an internship and placement with international organisations.

The 3rd Tier looks at local ICT training centres with proven training record. They should be in good standing with respect to their tax payments and industry best practice. This tier will receive funding in the form of grants and loan guarantees for equipments, capacity building and the subsidy for tuition. Funding to the tier should be part grant and part long-term loan. Due to the nature of the environment, there should be strong monitoring of the tier to ensure profitable growth and maturity.

## Management of the Fund

This fund should be managed by a Ministry of Science and Technology with strong collaboration with a Ministry of local Government and Rural Development (MLGRD). Since the fund would be channeled through district assemblies, it is important to use the MLGRD which has control and direct leverage with Assemblies. To use a different route might lead to the creation of another body with its attendant costs. Moreover, since the programme would have nationwide outreach, Assemblies are spread enough to cover the nation.

## Neighbourhood ICT Training Centres

Many of you are not privileged to be in school; neither are all second cycle institutions 'blessed' with an ICT centre. This shortcoming calls for the necessity of supporting ICT centres in all second cycle institutions. Furthermore, Neighbourhood ICT Training Centres should be encouraged within communities. These centres should have the capacity to train you outside formal training centres in basic computer skills to the level which would make you efficient in general endeavours. Those of you in the formal educational system could join though. There could be three options under the programme.

These are:

1. Publicly funded
2. Privately funded and
3. Public and Private sector partnership (the so-called PPP)

Funding under the public option could go as far as providing free facilitation by employing roving-trainers within zones and districts (counties).

The cost of learning material could be considered though. This could have two benefits. The first is giving opportunity to the youth who are without the benefit of ICT centres in their schools and those with interest in ICT related profession to have a foothold. The other benefit is that, it accords those with basic skills to further pursue training at a higher level. District Assemblies should encourage and support ICT centres across their jurisdictions.

It is important to consider ICT as a profession in its loftiness and not as an avenue for social networking and (or) other surf practices. ICT could be a gold mine for the nation. India makes over Three Billion US dollars (USD 3, 000,000,000.00) annually from software development, the United States makes over Twelve Billion US dollars (USD 12, 000, 000,000.00) annually from ICT.

The case of Google, Intel, IBM, Oracle, Apple and Huawei brings in billions of dollars to their home economies. Ghana, South Africa, Nigeria, Ivory Coast or Rwanda might not make a billion from ICT but with a good attempt, we can make our hundreds of millions. And in the process, create thousands of jobs for our youth.

There is no way that we cannot compete to get our share of the global market. Even domestic consumption alone would be worth hundreds of millions. Not to mention intra-trade among African nations.

We should take ICT serious beyond rhetoric. For example, Rwanda has an ambitious programme to make the country the 'Singapore of Africa'. The programme is in the third phase now. It started in 2000. The first phase ran up to 2005, with the aim of creating sustainable favourable conditions for ICT environment.

The second phase concentrated on building ICT backbone and fibre optic cables and the third which runs from 2011 to 2015 aims at harvesting by speeding of services to exploit the benefits of ICT from government, individual and corporate points of view in order to achieve an ICT culture within the spheres of the country's commercial life. In this regard, the government plans to build and strengthen ICT training centres.

The steps taken are worth mentioning. There are other plans on the drawing board by many African countries. I guess the point is to take a step beyond the drawing board. We need the political will and the commitment to ICT development and employment on the continent. The infrastructural framework is slow in coming to life.

I strongly recommend that, you pursue ICT beyond the basic level. ICT has enormous job opportunities and those pursuing professional lives in it would not regret it. ICT cuts across banking, agriculture, the services sector, and indeed almost any industry that comes to mind. Note that beyond acquiring the technical know-how, innovation and creativity are essential to surviving in the industry.

In this light, the government ought to commit to training large number of you in the areas of information and communication technology to broaden your range of opportunities and make you marketable on the international market.

As usual, note that, governments would have to be 'reminded' to readily implement a wide-ranging and a realistic ICT programme. In reminding the government, you would have to make sound and realistic proposal to help polish the programmes. The programmes should have depth and breadth. It should be quality enough to match the standard required by industry.

In the light of this, the following programmes are proposed:

1. The institution of an Annual Intra-District ICT Competition, opened to students and none student

2. Inter-District ICT Competition among Districts in the region

3. Annual Inter-Regional ICT Competition

4. Inter-University ICT Competition

5. National ICT Week

6. National ICT competition. The best ten ideas to be selected for support and funding

7. Institution of Municipal, Regional and National ICT Incubation Centres to provide space and technical advice to ICT initiatives

8. Annual National and International Technology Fairs to showcase new technologies, and futuristic ideas (ICT trend forecasting)

9. Intra-Bloc (Eg: ECOWAS, SADC and East African... ICT Competition)

10. Inter Bloc ICT Competition (Annual African ICT Entre-preneurial Competition)

In all these, there should be an award scheme which would include a seed capital and scholarship to train at an African

University in ICT. It could also be arranged for the winners to have internship at a global ICT firm. Additionally, those of you with entrepreneurial drive should be encouraged to set-up business under an Incubation Centre.

We have the opportunities to create a solid platform for our youth. It is important we take advantage of the enthusiasms of energetic, innovative and forward-looking youth and give them a hand. We must not fail them.

## ICT In Focus: The Case Of Rwanda

> When a nation overcomes her demons and makes peace with her past; when a nation finds her soul and establishes her destiny, she shall rise and when she does, she rises to the skies with hope and purpose...

The ANANSE VERSES Chapter 1:53:1

After the unfortunate horrors of 1994, the world and even much of Africa expected Rwanda to sink deeper into chaos and unravel into a failed state. We were all wrong. Today, that is not the story of Rwanda. It is an African story of true leadership, vision and the hard and difficult choices President Kagame and his team made to develop a knowledge based economy with ICT as the driving force amidst competing priorities. Without major natural resources or a large population to encourage a consumption-based economy, it forged ahead with a simple but deeper dream; ICT for Development (ICT4D).

Rwanda's ICT programme is bold, focused and comes with depth. Perhaps, it is one of the few countries on the continent which is walking the talk on using ICT as the new goldmine, the new frontier. The ICT project in Rwanda is no longer a proposal on paper nor a vision. It is a work very much on a transformational journey. A vision I hope for many African nations.

The overall vision is to use ICT as a tool for socio-economic development to fast-track Rwanda's transition into a middle-income country by 2020 and thus becoming the regional ICT Hub. Like the dream of many an African nation, and proven in South Korea, Taiwan and elsewhere, ICT is a powerful tool for development and a source of great wealth.

In Rwanda, most ICT investments have come from the Private sector - owing to an ever-improving environment for doing business. Rwanda ranks 32 globally today. However, the Government has been making important investments from its core budget to build infrastructure.

The ICT programme is under five priority areas, namely

1. The Governance Sector
2. The Health Sector
3. The Education Sector
4. The Agriculture sector and
5. The Business & Finance Sector,

## *Investments and Achievements*

1. The government has attracted three national carriers; MTN Rwanda, Tigo Rwanda and Airtel Rwanda which operate competitively to deliver data and voice services at affordable prices.

2. Increase in Mobile Phone subscribers to 65% to enhance mobile platform transactions. The African average is 80%. Kenya is at 71% and Nigeria, 94%.

3. The government, through a World Bank project, has been able to purchase Bulk Internet bandwidth from Uganda and Tanzania, which has allowed additional 2.4 Gbps, thus increasing available Internet bandwidth to 3.5Gbps.

4. Availability of a National Data Centre with a new cloud computing platform to centrally host Public and Private sector applications and services. (Rwanda is among the very few countries with highly available, resilient and robust data centre infrastructure on the continent, and will position the country to offer very stable online services.)

5. Rwanda was ranked the most dynamic African country in the ITU ICT Development Index (IDI), in the ITU "Measuring the Information Society 2012."

6. The incorporation of a company, Broadband Systems Corporation (BSC), to commercialize the National Fibre Optic Backbone, the Kigali Metropolitan Network and the National Data Centre which was launched in May 2012. BSC provides data services to Government institutions and sells excess capacity to Telecom Operators at a cheaper market costs.

7. The Government invested in laying out a national Fibre Optic Backbone that reaches all the 30 districts of the country and 9 border posts. In total, more than 4500 km of fibre were deployed as both underground and overhead power transmission lines.

8. Another important investment is in ICT for education whereby as part of the One Laptop Per Child Program, the Government has so far distributed more than 200,000 to more than 400 primary schools around the country.

9. Several new Government to Business (G2B) and Government to Citizens (G2C) Services have been launched, including:

   a. There is an ePayment system, which allows citizens to pay their taxes online through their banks, hence reducing queues and delivery time. This is part of the e-tax system, which allows citizens to e-file their taxes using even their mobile phones to carry out their tax declaration. This system which used to be on quarterly and monthly basis is now executed on real time basis using electronic billing machines, which are linked to the tax administration. The other side of the story is that, the ICT side of the system is managed and maintained by Rwandans, most of whom are the youth.

b.  There is also the Single Electronic Window System, a facility that allows parties involved in trade and transport to lodge standardized information and documents with a single entry point to fulfil all import, export, and transit-related regulatory requirements, hence reducing the cost of doing business due to online clearance and allowing simplified procedures.

10. The Carnegie Mellon University (CMU) campus at their Telecom House was rehabilitated and its campus was launched in August 2012. The first intake of students for the 2012-2013 academic year of the Masters programme has a total of 24 students. The emphasis is not on the number of students but the fact that, a world class College is training students at the postgraduate level in a core knowledge area critical in driving a knowledge economy forward.

11. The establishment of kLab (knowledge Lab) as the first ever "ICT Innovation Centre" in the country and made operational. kLab, is a technology space (a form of Incubation Centre), which brings like-minded innovators together and give them the resources they need to explore their ideas, learn from each other, and develop innovative ICT solutions. kLab is a technology space enabling ambitious entrepreneurs come together and develop their trailblazing ideas into successful businesses.

On the health front, the following has been achieved:

12. The percentage of health facilities with functional infrastructure (computer, Internet, including modems) reached 84%. This allows the health facilities to access health information systems and medical records systems and provide better and timely reporting.

In a bid to improve and open governance, I noticed the following milestones:

13. The installation of Access Points (2 per sectors), which are fully owned and managed by relevant administrative districts. With consideration to the existing Business Development Centres, these access points are now totalling to 91 Access Points, providing Business Plans, ICT trainings and access to online information and services.

14. Document Tracking was deployed in 25 institutions (with almost all ministries) and currently being deployed for 40 additional institutions (that includes all provinces & districts). This automated tool will allow sensible reduction of paper usage in Government. It also speeds up processes. This is more or less a paperless government.

15. Rwanda has Automated Passenger Clearance System, a system that support the automation of the migration services rendered to border communities and airports and streamlines data uniformly to enhance speed and efficiency of operations. Additionally, there is also the Biometric data, which removes the need for human input and passport stamps, reduces the migration clearance processing time, eliminates risks of fraud and detects use of illegal and forged documents.

16. In Rwanda, a total of 7 institutions which are connected to the National Identification Authority Database use online secure authentication, namely Traffic Police, RRA, MTN, TIGO, AIRTEL, B.N.R /Credit Reference Bureau, Immigration. Through this secure access, these institutions are able to provide better and quicker services to their constituencies.

Finally on Agriculture Sector:

17. There is an eSoko system, which has empowered farmers by giving them timely access to price information. The system currently undertakes nearly 100,000 transactions.

18. There is also the Fertilizer Voucher Management System which has issued more than 120,000 fertilization vouchers, allowing nearly 3 million farmers to benefit from the fertilizers distribution countrywide.

## Challenges

1. Low electricity penetration, which makes the use of conventional gadget challenging.

2. Low per capita.

3. Low purchasing power, which makes it difficult for consumers to afford data and apps and hardware.

4. Low Internet penetration of 20%. African average for Internet penetration, according to ITU is at 15.3%.

5. Low digital appreciation and literacy.

## *Tackling the challenges*

On the electricity challenge, The ICT Minister, Jean Philbert, tells me, 'We have learned to use off-grid, low cost solutions such as pre-paid solar power systems.' He went on to add, 'We have launched the first Solar Powered Internet School in East Africa in partnership with Samsung Electronics. On the economic front, we have learned to make ICT solutions affordable. The government has promoted schemes that allow consumers to acquire smart devices and pay them in instalments for instance.'

'On the digital literacy, we have learned that Government alone cannot do the job, so we are working with the Private sector and Civil Society Organisations, especially Faith Based Organisations to promote not only basic literacy but also digital literacy.' This feed into the now popular idea of Private Public Partnership (PPP).

The government has 'several partnerships with global software powerhouses - an example is Facebook with which we developed a program called SocialEDU that extends social networking experience to academic learning.' The program aims at reaching 20,000 students in Rwanda. Nokia, Airtel and EdEx are also part of the same partnership. Building relationship with big corporations could be painstaking but once it is established, it guarantees benefits on many fronts. It helps government to tap into the resources of the corporations as much as it offers the government access to the best brains there are.

## Conclusion

The foregoing narrative is not about the scale of achievements of Rwanda but the vision, commitment and the responsibilities the government has imposed upon itself. The nation, after 1994, has moved on to reach milestones. There is tenacity and purposefulness many an African youth expects their governments to possess.

From the Rwanda ICT4D experience, one senses a real commitment to an agenda, which is purposefully being pursued; and hopefully I wish many an African nation took on a more ambitious vision. British app developers are expected to bring in revenues exceeding £4 Billion this year alone. It is a field worth whatever investment governments pumped in. Many an African nation is doing well but largely on paper. There should be much direct efforts from governments in the areas of providing infrastructure and creating the right environment. My call is for direct intervention by government by promoting and investing in ICT infrastructure and building the necessary networks for the youth to thrive.

# 10

## Youth Employment, Skills Training and Entrepreneurship

*"Today's young people are the best-educated and trained generation ever. In terms of employment, the expected inflow of young people into the labour market, rather than being viewed as a problem, should be recognised as presenting an enormous opportunity and potential for economic and social development."*

Juan Somavia, Director-General, ILO, Interviewed by the Financial Times, 23rd January 2010

## Comments

The African youth unemployment question is close to exploding. It is sad and disappointing to see university graduates selling dog chains, cleaning factory floors and doing all sorts of menial jobs. According to the World Bank, the youth accounts for 60% of all unemployed in Africa; nearly 40 million people. Additionally, according to the African Economic Outlook, 'On average, more than 70% of Africa's youth live on less than US$2 per day.' African leaders seem to be aware of this with actions being taken on many fronts. In many countries such as Ghana, Senegal, Nigeria, Ethiopia and Zimbabwe, it has become hot button election issues.

Sections of the youth are innovating. Some research puts 'self employed youth in the Democratic Republic of the Congo, Ethiopia, Ghana, Malawi, Mali, Rwanda, Senegal and Uganda at 60%'. This observation seems encouraging but it is worth adding that, many of these jobs are menial and below the levels of training of these youth. It is estimated that, about '10 million to 12 million young people join the labour market each year.' Yet concrete, sustained and meaningful steps towards meeting the employment challenge of these skilled youth remains elusive.

The African Youth Decade (2009 - 2018) Plan of Action, adopted on the 26th of July, 2006 in Banjul was in recognition of the need for urgent action on the youth unemployment saga. Since then, modest steps have been taken by some governments to provide employment opportunities for the youth. In Ghana, the government created the Ghana Youth Employment and Entrepreneurship Agency (GYEEDA), which according to the 2010 budget statement, has created one hundred and ten thousand, seven hundred and ninety-six (110,796) jobs for the youth, a paltry 20% of its target.

With the proposed establishment of the National Youth Employment Programme Fund, it is hoped that access to funding would enhance the expansion of the programme as we also wait for the steps to ensure the quality and sustainability of the programme to take shape.

According to the UN, Mauritius has developed a plan to encourage technical and vocational education for young people. Zambia has also introduced 'a national youth policy and a youth enterprise fund to stimulate job creation'. The Nigerian government introduced a 'skills acquisition and enterprise development programme as a component of the existing national youth service corps; it also introduced a business plan competition dubbed *YouWin*, which grants winners start-up financing'. Cote d'Ivoire has the AIFPA, with the 'objective of establishing the system of the initial vocational training and apprenticeship in certain work-linked occupations. This means that, young persons have greater chances of lasting and sustainable employment. Namibia, among others, have the Katutura Youth Enterprise Centre (KAYEC) Scheme with the aim of helping the 'youth develop the attitudes, knowledge and skills needed for productive work (employment or self-employment) by providing non-formal vocational skills training for self-employment'.

These are modest steps but obviously not enough. According to the International Labour Organization (ILO) between 2000 and 2008, Africa created an estimated '73 million jobs, but only 16 million for young people aged between 15 and 24.'

Africa has an enormous opportunity 'with almost 200 million people aged between 15 and 24', this figure is the youngest population in the world. This gives an indication of a young labour force for the labour markets. Irrespective of this, there is the likelihood that the attitude of most African governments to youth job creation would turn this opportunity into a nightmare.

According to the McKinsey Global Institute at a 2.7%, by 2040, the continents labour force (Between 15-64 years) is estimated to be '1 billion strong surpassing both China and India' and the largest in the world. By 2045, the World Bank estimates that, 'With almost 200 million people aged between 15 and 24, Africa has the youngest population in the world.' At even the current rate, this 'number of young people in Africa will double by 2045.' This should light a fire under the comfortable seats of many African leaders to rise up and tap into this enormous opportunity rather than allow it to become a nightmare of continental proportions. With this raw resource of youth, Africa does not need gold, oil, platinum and bauxite to become a global powerhouse. With vision, focus and planning, we can create a global workforce out of these youth. Our youth, with their energy, drive and enthusiasm, should be our gold and diamonds.

The issue of lack of skills or education can also no longer be an excuse. According to the UN, 'Africa's youth population is not only growing rapidly; it is also getting better educated.' Furthermore, '59% of 20-24 year olds will have had secondary education in 2030'. In simple terms, this will translate into 137 million young persons within the ages of 20-24 'with secondary education and 12 million with tertiary education in 2030.' Clearly, these 'trends offer an unrivalled opportunity for economic and social development if the talents of this swiftly increasing reservoir of human capital are harnessed and channelled towards the productive sectors of the economy'. The above notwithstanding, if African leaders do not plan well, it could be another missed opportunity which this time around would lead to the unravelling of many nations. The fundamental question is: Would African leaders take up this opportunity which Europe would kill for? We are witnessing how China is tapping into its youth force. On annual basis, China is training more than hundred thousand (100,000) engineers alone.

We have no option than to tap into this gold mine of energetic, enthusiastic and skilled labour force. We should take to manufacturing and value addition to our vast base of raw materials. We should further pursue a knowledge-based economy, which has a proven basis for success.

Besides all else, it is expected that we should encourage entrepreneurship among our youth. When is Africa waking up? When is Africa going to sit up and be there for her youth? These are questions our youth is asking. These are questions African politicians must answer.

### Back to Basics; a note from Industry

Industries have not expanded fast and large enough to absorb the large number of youth leaving school for life. Besides capacity, industries have two complaints with respect to graduates. First, they contend graduates are not of the right calibre they require. Your academic training is industrially inadequate. And two, government policies, punitive taxes and high energy cost among others are stunting growth. Government on one hand blames industry for poor management and lack of proactive drive and focus. Students, on one hand, rightly complain there are no jobs. No white collar jobs in the tradition they have been trained to expect in the real world.

According to estimates from the International Labour Organization, more than one hundred million new jobs would have to be created within the next twenty years in order to provide suitable employment for the growing number of young people in the economically active populations of developing countries. African leaders must meet this challenge. It seems the job for most African leaders have been cut for them.

The situation of girls and young women, that of young people with 'disabilities, refugee youth, displaced persons, street children, indigenous youth, migrant youth and minorities warrants urgent attention.

Considering the above bare bone situation, the solution to the issues is far above the youth. We require immediate, medium and long-term solutions, which would bring forth realistic solutions. The short-term recommendations would include specific programmes targeted at the youth to enhance their skills levels, job market orientation and to a large extent, inculcate in them the cultures of innovation and entrepreneurship. Within the medium to the long-term, the focus should be on growing, strengthening and diversifying our economies. Our economies need drastic fundamental reorganisation to make them agile. The norm of depending on primary and extractive metals and raw materials as the drivers of economic growth is most reckless and unsustainable. We need proven methodologies of growth. In this light, among many others, we need three (3) drastic measures:

1. Reorganisation of our economies to migrate from primary product base to manufacturing and services.

2. Enhancing the business environment to make it conducive for the private sector to thrive so that, they can expand and absorb the large pool of youth joining the workforce. Obviously, creating jobs for 7-10 million young persons is a daunting task. Pet youth programmes would not suffice. The larger economy would have to be structured to suit the youth and create jobs.

3. Promoting entrepreneurship among the youth, supporting them with grants, long-term low interest loan facilities and internships. Furthermore, they need the attitudes and behaviours necessary to survive the job market.

## The Street Youth and Minimum Skills Test

There is no doubt that, the street-youth have become both a burden and a threat, hence requiring politicians to take a hard look at their plight. In order to prepare the street-youth to be useful for national development, it would be important for such youth to acquire the basic skills of reading, writing and communication before they are allowed into the real world so that they can productively take part in the life of the society.

Thus, apprenticeship schemes, NVTI, and the STEP programmes should be expanded to include this class of the youth for them to follow their dreams and make them useful contributors to our national efforts.

It should be noted that it is through employment that young people can realize their aspirations, improve their living conditions and fulfil their responsibilities, not only as productive agents but also as citizens.

Towards the achievement of this aim, it is important to strengthen existing programmes. Additionally, we should strengthen basic education to enhance its quality so that graduates terminating from it acquire the three essential skills of reading, writing and communication as well as relevant job skills which would enable them to be employable or be prepared for higher learning.

It is important to accredit private sector institutions, under guidelines, to support the Informal Education Programmes to implement the programme. In this way, the burden of start-up cost would be on the private sector and not the government. With the government outside the bracket of delivery, it would have the liberty and concentration to monitor and supervise the programme.

Getting employment in the informal sector is not just securing a job or growing the same. In order to turnout prepared youth onto the job market, it is important to put in a necessary assessment scheme that would assess the ability to survive the turbulent job market, start, grow and integrate their businesses into the formal sector. In this drive, there is the need for every youth dropping out of school to enter the job market prior to secondary education, to sit for Minimum Skills Test.

The Minimum Skills Test should examine the following:
1. Ability to read
2. Ability to write

3.  Ability to communicate in English (optional)

4.  Certified Graduate Of A Job Based Skill. For example, in areas such as dressmaking, carpentry, masonry, fabrication and any other necessary skills stipulated by the NYA. This test should not be administered by the Ghana Education Service. The NVTI, or National Youth Authority, should be authorised to conduct the assessment. This test should be uniform and mandatory.

5.  It should test among others, literacy, mathematics, basic commerce, orientation to national development, patriotism and culture.

It is important to note that, Basic School graduates can have direct entry onto the job market if they pass a Basic Education Certificate Examination (BECE).

Funding for skills training towards the Minimum Skills Test should be regular and sustained. This would make sure that, managers could plan, integrate programmes and implement the same without constraints. For this reason, the government should introduce Skills Development Levy to pay for the training programmes.

A levy of 5% on selected luxury goods including luxury cars, all alcoholic products, cigarettes, cigars, high fuel consumption vehicles ( beyond 3.0 engine capacity) of non medical or scientific field. Professional sports cars should be exempted. All cosmetic products for the skin, nails, eyes and any other part of the body should be included. High-end 3.5G smart phones should also be considered. Well, it is only an appeal to those who can afford to spend One Thousand Five Hundred Ghana

Cedis (GHC1, 500.00) on a cell phone (about a thousand US dollars) to contribute say 0.1% of the amount towards skills training. Revenues from this levy should be extended to support vocational training. This would enhance an existing or yet to be established Skills development Fund.

Furthermore, it is worth considering redirecting the Non-formal Education (NFE) to more effectively cover the youth than the aged. Their current programmes cover ages, fifteen (15) to forty-five (45). Despite this specification, in reality it is more of a programme for the aged than for the youth. 'Non-formal education' classes are filled with middle aged women and in some cases have no single youth in attendance (This is the finding of a six month survey of seven centres).

This is not to suggest that, educational resources should be the sole preserve of the youth. Rather, in the sphere of limited resources, it is prudent to spend on the youth than the aged who have limited opportunities and time space to contribute to the society. Any individual beyond the youth bracket wishing for formal education should be ready to fund his own 'education'.

Teachers and facilitators already working on the NFE should be asked to stay on to direct those of you who would join the programme. That is to say, the existing management structure of the NFE should not be altered beyond directing the programme to cater solely for the youth. The only change would be the 'students'.

Training centres, allowances and administrative staff should be maintained. In this direction, issues of course material, time-table could be modified to reflect on the new paradigm.

On the other hand, in order not to leave the middle aged who could not afford private tuition out, it is important to urge Student Unions and resident educationists to take their education on a voluntary basis within their communities.

An educated and trained youth is a prerequisite for development and a secured means of laying a solid foundation for the future. So is such an enlightenment needed for a successful life and to a large extent, for entrepreneurial success. It is important to note that, a literate (ability to read, write and communicate) youth in business with the right orientation is by and large, likely to grow into an international entity and integrate into the formal sector than an illiterate class. He is more likely to look beyond the national boundary than the 'timid' youth limited by his inadequate knowledge and outlook. The emphasis here is to afford the youth certain key skills and for them to appreciate the need for higher skills in their endeavours. That is to say, with these basic skills they stand a good chance of adding to their knowledge through self education and even through the formal structure at a later stage in life.

The assumption is that, with the knowledge and skills they would grow their businesses beyond levels they would have had without formal knowledge in business and related programmes. That is not to say illiterates cannot succeed in business. We cannot equate illiteracy with knowledge. Their illiteracy is denoted by their inability to read and write. This does not mean they are not knowledgeable.

Thus, to equate their inability to read and write as empty headedness is a smack of ignorance, and whoever is caught in this flawed thinking should have to reconsider his position. There has been a keen observation as to who holds the resources of the nation in the informal private sector. It is not the graduates, or suit wearing class. Largely, the informal sector is populated by 'illiterates' who hold sway on capital,

135

and large resources. The situation is considerable and requires much attention, considering the fact that some commentators put the size of the informal economy at as much as sixty percent (60%) of the formal sector across the continent. As such the informal sector, relative to the 'illiterate' class, ought to be considered in-depth and broadly. So that in creating jobs, both informal and formal sectors ought to be considered. The emphasis is to broaden their outlook and horizon.

## 'Kayayei (Head Porters), Dog Chain Sellers and Minimum Skills Test

The position of 'kayayei' (head porters), 'dog chain sellers', apprentices in carpentry shops, seamstresses, basic school dropouts and other 'traffic-light' entrepreneurs should be accorded a special mention. That is to say, more importantly, this category should be included in the Minimum Skills Test programme. For this reason, government ought to make the necessary sacrifices to bring this important constituency into mainstream formal or quasi-formal sectors towards national development.

Towards the realisation of this policy, the government should propose humane, pragmatic, and reasonable programmes to implement this policy. Suffice to say, if the right approach is not taken, this lofty intention would backfire in the face of any government willing to undertake this delicate issue.

The reasons and benefits therefrom, should be clearly emphasised so that, the programme does not become a victim of misconception. Thus, it would be seen as a tool for denying the informal sector youth the opportunity for livelihood by asking them to educate and integrate. Consequently, this could be a costly political venture.

It is important to recognise that, this class of youth survives by themselves and to a large extent, many of them have dependents. As such, to ask them off the streets during the course of training and to deny them basic allowances would break the scheme apart.

Towards planning for the youth, it is important to collect their database or borrow it from any existing data. Understandably, without knowing the number of unemployed youth, their geographic distribution, aspirations and migration, it would be difficult to formulate policies and conceive the same to effect the intended policy. In 2001, the then government, fresh from electoral victory attempted a similar exercise unilaterally without broad based consultation and I should say the result was a disaster.

In successfully considering the education and integration of the street-youth, three benefits are at the heart of the matter. Firstly we would put a halt to excessive expansion of the informal economy by depriving the sector of fresh supply of personnel. In this light, as the current sector is integrated into the mainstream, there would not be the need to commit resources in courting new class of informal business class into the formal economy. This would lead to better planning and revenue mobilisation.

Secondly, we would tend to use the integration of this existing informal sector as an example that the formal sector offers better returns for entrepreneurs through benefits such as tax breaks, technical resources, facilitations and relevant representations. For that matter, the government has to plan effectively to cater for their entrepreneurial and commercial needs. We need them to be identified, file their tax returns, and use official channels in their endeavours. Furthermore, they would be urged to cut all ties with black market dealers and underground operators in their respective businesses.

Thirdly, it is understandable that, the large informal sector does not only make it difficult for fiscal and policy planning. It also takes a bit from revenue mobilisation. It is, therefore, important to acknowledge that, critical thinking and resources ought to be committed to the reduction of the size of the sector. When this is achieved, it is hoped that we could plan better and increase revenue mobilisation.

### Kayayei: Head Porters

Estimates put the number of Kayayei at fifty thousand (50,000) across the country. Largely, they are migratory youth who have moved to commercial centres in search of better economic conditions. Kayayei consists of seven categories. These include:

1.  *New Comers*: These are the newly arrived in the cities for work. They usually have no place to stay and as such are open to a whole lot of challenges.

2.  *Receivers*: These are the benevolent and /or 'family' members who accept to watch over the newly arrived. They act as their protectors. Usually, they take not more than three (3) new arrivals.

3.  *Mothers*: They are the oldies and long staying members of the community. They are the people who resolve disputes and challenges facing members.

4.  *Sisters*: The sisters are village members who have met

138

in the centres either by accident or design. They walk, sleep and do almost everything together.

5.  *Territorial Owners*: They control territories and could decide who works in a territory or not. Usually, their control is for peaceful and communal purposes. They usually decide accommodation. Furthermore, they liaise with store owners to arrange mat spaces for accommodation.

6.  *Bosses*: These are normally the male manipulators. They are abusive and exploitative. Usually they are truck pushers but share territory with the Kayayei. They are only nice to their 'lovers' and sexual benefactors.

7.  *Masses*: These are those who have learnt to survive without any alliances. They do not look for favours and give none.

## Daily Challenges

1.  Lack of accommodation.

2.  Sexual abuse through forced sex and rape.

3.  Financial exploitation by bosses.

4.  Physical abuse through beating.

5.  Mental abuse by hirers for non-payment of agreed porting fees.

6.  White-theft by store owners and mothers who volunteer to keep daily earnings.

7.  Robbery by thieves.

Towards the realisation of getting the Kayayei the basic skills in reading, writing and communication, government should propose humane, pragmatic, and reasonable programmes to implement this policy. Suffice to say, if the right approach is not taken, this lofty intention would backfire in the face of any government willing to undertake this delicate issue.

## Dog Chain Sellers/Traffic Light Entrepreneurs

The case of dog chain sellers and traffic light entrepreneurs follows a similar structure with the exception that, their migratory route into mainstream entrepreneurial activity is more rigorous and secured. These entrepreneurs have a large success rate which is normally within 3-5years. They are more purposeful and forceful. The reasons and benefits therefrom, should be clearly emphasised so that, the programme does not become a victim of misconception. Thus, it would be seen as a tool for denying the informal sector youth the opportunity for livelihood by asking them to educate and integrate.

Consequently, this could be a costly political venture. It is important to recognise that, this class of youth survives by themselves and to a large extent, many of them have dependents. As such, to ask them off the streets during the course of training and to deny them basic allowances would break the scheme apart. This is a highly vulnerable group and unorganised. As such, youth leaders are supposed to champion their course on their behalf.

## *A National Youth Authority and Temporal Training Centre*

The collection of such a data could be done better by involving the Statistical Services, the NYA, Student Unions and other stakeholders who would have the capacity to secure accurate data.

By decentralising the registration exercise to the District/ Provincial levels, the government would increase efficiency. Furthermore, STEPs centres, NVTIs and any other programme should be consolidated to implement the programmes intended to facilitate the policy of successfully integrating the 'kayayei and under-the-traffic light entrepreneurs. NVTI centres or Temporary Training Centres should be used to cater for the assessment exercise. Most appropriately, the Technical Vocational Education and Training (TVET) could also expand its capacity to administer the programme.

Furthermore, participants in the most vulnerable enclaves should be given priority to ensure that they are not left behind. Even as they are undergoing skills training, they should be given the opportunity to benefit from the minimum skill test programme. What is being advocated is that, there would be some candidates who would need government support in preparing for the basic minimum skills test. This is to say that, candidates could train with accredited centres at no cost to them. In order to ensure the success of the programme in the face of recent economic hardship, the cost of training and assessment should be borne by government.

Additionally, District Assemblies could pay allowances to trainees on per day basis as much as they would earn in a day on the streets. Considering the cost of such a position, it would be necessary to consider the programmes on a part-time basis. In this manner, the youth could go to work and come to 'school' later in the day.

Government should consider offering incentives in the form of equipments, workspaces and loan guarantees through Microfinance Institutions and other financial agencies with expertise in microloans, for those who are willing to go ahead to learn beyond the basic skill level to acquire hard skills needed for harnessing higher opportunities in the society.

On the question of infrastructure, existing school and public premises could be used without disrupting government expenditure plans.

## Projecting For The Future

In the current environment, you have little chance of gaining meaningful high earned employment to meet your aspirations and dreams. Our industrial base to create room for employment is small and weak. Our private sector to absorb graduating youth is undersized and our public sectors have aging personnel who are refusing to give way by either undercutting their age and securing extensions under contracts or staying put with impunity. Even more disturbing is the fact that, our tertiary educational system has not changed or has been slow in changing to meet the demands of fast expanding sectors of commerce, ICT and services.

Our streets are fraught with unemployed youth with the skills and academic qualifications. The sad aspect is the fact that, even those with sound business plans and possess entrepreneurial skills cannot secure the necessary support to pursue their dreams.

142

On projecting for the future, there is the need for all classes of youth to be catered for to help them acquire the life skills necessary for them to survive without making them a burden to the larger society. More importantly, beyond skills, government should support them to start-up in life and their aspirational endeavours.

## Characteristics of Effective Youth Training Programmes

*(Adopted from the United Nations Youth Charter)*

1. Flexibility and responsiveness to the needs of the workplace

2. Links with the labour market and employers

3. Internship programmes through partnerships with local businesses

4. An emphasis on personal development and career planning

5. On-the-job training and work-study programmes

6. Inclusion of those who work in the informal economy or those who have never been employed

7. Entry requirements that permit informal workers and people from historically disadvantaged groups to participate and benefit

8. Opportunities for mentoring and the exchange of information among peers

9. Vocational guidance that does not discriminate against or stereotype young women

## A Council for Technical and Vocational Education and Training

It is commendable that, a Council for Technical and Vocational Education and Training (COTVET) is created to coordinate the activities of technical institutions. This is necessary to ensure that, the informal apprentice training centres, constituting nearly 70% of apprenticeship training across many countries, is systematically brought into the formal educational fold.

Coordination though is not enough to adequately cater for technical institutions or address the far-reaching technical revolution being advocated. Suffice to say, the need for reconciliation of technical institutions to run coherent programmes synchronised for uniformity and with a greater role in developing its own programmes is critical to the development of technical education. Additionally, COTVET should conduct regular review of programmes and monitor to ensure that coordination among technical institutions is maintained.

In this vein, private carpentry businesses should be encouraged to support vocational training programmes. In Ghana, companies like Akuaba, Agorwu and Kpogas have well defined management and technical structures to accept interns. A link should be established with such businesses.

Supervision is also critical in the pursuit of effective vocational training institutions. Additionally, it is important to address the breadth and depth of the programmes without affecting their span and quality.

# 11

## National Service Scheme and Job Centres

*'Dedicate yourself to the welfare of your nation. There is not greater service than this'*

Unknown

## Comments

You ought to understand that, as on many other issues, you have an enormous say when it comes to the employment issue. On the issue of unemployment, it is necessary to strengthen the bond between you and other stakeholders, especially employers. This is also to underscore the need for the expansion of the economy through investment and business friendly programmes. Besides unemployment being traditionally and relatively attributed to factors such as growth and lack of appropriate skills, it is important to look at the institutional and (or) programmes side of unemployment.

A National Youth Authority in consultation with school counsellors and existing youth programmes should endeavour to ensure that you have the best advice and information on employment paths available to you per your course areas, abilities and interests. Note that, you are intellectually competent to make proposals relative to unemployment and other programmes affecting you.

In pursuit of this, school authorities should create desk officers to man this portfolio to ensure that, students are saved the tortuous venture of career choices relative to their aspirations and programmes with high employment rates. It is important not to use this desk as a tool for stereotyping by 'forcing' students into certain perceived areas. For instance, coaching women into catering and drama jobs or home economics against their wish is unhealthy and has long term consequences. The emphasis is that, available options should be made known to them regarding future professions.

## *National Service Scheme: Should it be extended by A Year?*

With a huge backlog of unemployed youth, coupled with the enormous assistance National Service personnel offer to industry during their service, it is expedient to consider the extension of the National Service Scheme to three years; one year mandatory and the second and third years optional. This should include the aggressive expansion of the service Scheme to the private informal sector for them to take up a portion of graduates. This would bring up traditional benefit of learning and bring new expertise to the sector.

Additionally, this development would help foster confidence and build trust between the informal sector and formal sector where graduates are traditionally trained to work.

As an incentive, central government could absorb 30% of allowances due service personnel without levying any cost on the private sector as the case is today. This may invariably ignite the process of recruiting more graduates. It may be a long way off with challenges in areas such as remuneration and attitude. The argument is not to say that, the solution to graduate unemployment is the building of trust between graduates and the informal sector.

Graduates need to appreciate the opportunities in the sector and begin to explore ways of tapping into the potential of this large sector. It could also prop them up from the underground into the mainstream economy. This would come with other consequent benefits such as increases in revenue generation and better planning. Obviously, issues of social security payments and appropriate remuneration levels would come up as immediate challenges.

## *Job Centres*

The issue of job centres with an online option would enhance the job search and security of the youth. That is to say, the government should establish job centres on campuses and commercial centres to facilitate youth job search. These offices of course should be open to both students and non-students. Or as an option, a multi-purpose job centre should be established in cities. That is to say, these centres should have a professional career coaches and mentors attached to them to offer round the clock advisory services. Jobs on this platform should not be restricted. Rather it should include full time, part-time, hourly jobs, skilled and unskilled.

At the job centres, attendants should be available to help job seekers search for the jobs online. Largely, the job centres should be online and integrated so that, a job seeker at Jobcentre 'A' can search through data on Jobcentre 'B' or on any location, unless the candidate is not qualified for the job.

For the purposes of cutting cost and uniformity of operations, it is important that the National Youth Authority or any appropriate agency can undertakes the task of coordinating with employers to identify job openings and make them available to the centre.

Direct access to the database of the job centre's site would pose a security risk due to the security certificates of many websites. This notwithstanding, appropriate secured channels should be established to ensure that job openings from industry or the public sector are made available to the job centres timely. Furthermore since the data would be online, any youth job seeker can access job opening from any internet café or even on their mobile phones.

The issue of communication between industry and the Jobcentre should be considered. Thus, hot phone lines should be established for the industry to communicate job openings directly to the database of the job centre. The telecommunication industry could facilitate by providing the centre with subsidized calls for the government on one hand, and free for job seekers on the other.

The other form of communication is for job seekers to make enquiries about jobs posting from the job centre premises free of charge. In this line, major cooperation would be required from the Telecom Companies.

# 12

## Skills Bridging Centre

*'Skills and Confidence are an Unconquered Army'*

George Herbert (3rd April 1593 – 1st March 1633) A Welsh-Born English Poet, Orator and Anglican Priest

## Comments

It is worth noting that, the lack of adequate symmetry between educational policy, practice and industry, paints a disturbing picture. It costs industries more to retrain graduates to fit into their respective jobs. Many a youth completes school and finds out that, you need more than certificates to pursue your dreams in Industry. Much of what you have been taught at school are more of an academic venture and less a realistic knowledge base sought after by industry. Thus, many of you are narrow in your knowledge and lack confidence. This is the stark reality many of you come to face in the real world of work and employment.

This weak fundamental at the terminal points of many educational systems threatens the dreams and aspirations of many of you wishing to pursue dreams in established corporations. For this reason, it is important for the government and industry to take a hard look at the situation. You have a responsibility to yourself to act, advisedly, through advocacy to get the government to sit down with Industry to resolve this.

In this light, it is necessary to set up a Skills Bridging Centre to specifically guide graduates to prepare them for the job market. This centre should not be another book gulping institution. It should be a facilitating centre. It should be a wholly practical knowledge centre with huge emphasis on gaining the right attitude. A graduate in Finance and Banking should be placed in a real world financial firm where he would be prepared before formally entering the job market. Industry should be encouraged to support the centre by taking candidates for placement. It would go a long way to cut their in-service training cost, since this time they have a partner in the government. In the light of this, industry should be involved throughout the preparation of the programme.

Thus, they should be seen as partners rather than supporters of the programme. The programme should be set up with the direct and active participation and control of industry. This is necessary because the 'graduates' from there more or less belong to them.

The Centre should not necessarily have training facilities of its own. It should coordinate with industry to make allowance for training for the participants on the programme. It could be in banking and finance, accountancy, furniture works, consultancy, metal fabrication, animal husbandry, planning, and as many industries as there are.

Furthermore, the centre should be staffed and headed by a non-political head whose appointment should be by a rigorous selection process supervised by industry.

## Duration Of The Programme

This leads us to the duration of the programme, training centres and funding. Three to five (3-5) months would be an ideal period for rigorous on the job training. The government should lead the process to get industry to sign onto the programme by accepting graduates for training. Participants should not bear any direct financial cost. This notwithstanding, administrative cost should be borne by both government and industry. The formula should be worked out so that none of the parties is disadvantaged.

It is important to state that, this interaction with industry could be used to identify 'high-demand skills' as required by industry and consequently, school curricula redesigned to reflect it. In other words, 'such partnerships can work to inform the school and training curricula and resource distribution channels according to the demands of major employers'. Such information would save the nation and school authorities resources. It is important to add that, School authorities and student leadership should be involved.

## Management of the Programme

One other area is the management of the centre. Three options come to mind. The first option is a single national body and the second option, regional based centres. A third option is having industry based centres. In this direction, a limited number of industries should be selected to begin the programme, say seven (7) industrial sectors.

Each of these options has its strengths and possible weaknesses. A single national coordinating centre would ensure uniformity in programme design and reduce cost. On the other hand, one single body managing a nationwide programme would face challenges in supervision and quality maintenance. The other challenge is the likelihood of abuse.

On the other hand, having ten regional based centres would do well for supervision even though all ten centres combined would need a larger budget for management. On the other hand, it would increase the efficiency. It would also increase the enthusiasm of participating industries since the localization of the programme would create a sense of ownership and proximity.

The third option is perhaps the most specific and simple. With this option, students in a particular industry, say banking, would register with the banking training centre to enrol on the programme. There are at least, two challenges here. If there are twenty industries, of which there are more, should it be that each region would have twenty centres? Secondly, if the programme is nationally based, should it be that a banking student in the Maranatha University College in Greater Accra Region would have to be at the national centre say in Kumasi or Ho to register and roll onto the programme?

Of the three, I would argue for a single national centre with slight modification. Considering the cost of managing ten centres, it would be difficult to fund the offices adequately. In this light, one centre with a very interactive website would suffice. That is, a student anywhere in the country who is selected could be sent an email or a text message concerning his placement. With this, regional education Directorates or any other well resourced agency should be encouraged to use their structures to help with supervision. Usually a Desk Office would suffice.

With the involvement of Universities, internet technology and all stakeholders (including student leadership), these nagging challenges could be better tackled to arrive at a programme with inputs from all stakeholders. The internet provides prompt and real time availability of information to participants of the programme. Thus websites, emails and text messages could be used as information in-and-out-flow channels.

## *Your Role And That Of Student Unions*

Stakeholders such as Student Unions could make inputs as to the implementation and running of the programme. Student Unions would provide a platform for raw inputs from students on the programme and would serve as reliable and low cost medium of information between students and the programme. Furthermore, they would serve as a link between students and the programme which is vital for ownership, trust and quality of the programme.

Universities have two obligations. The first is academic and the second, administrative. Universities need to seriously consider realigning course curricula to meet the areas of needs by industry both in breadth and depth. In the light of this need, close collaboration is most encouraged between the two. For instance, Annual Review Meetings (ARMs) with the trade unions, employers and industry players would lead to a better understanding of the needs and challenges confronting each arm.

The argument is not to call for the industrialisation of 'sacred' academic curricula. Rather, the argument is seeking to ensure that, universities train graduates who are ready and qualified for industry. Thus, the seller produces products the buyer is willing to buy. It is important to address this mismatch between what is thought at colleges and the intrinsic skill needs of industry if we are to help the youth in their transition from school to work.

The second obligation of Universities would involve the provision of basic student data such as names, course area, research area, contact address to the programme in a manner that would give cause for you, your parents or student groups to raise questions about privacy.

The underlining belief is that, there is the need for a national centre to facilitate your transition into industry. This singular objective should of course have challenges, but these challenges should spur us on as a nation rather than discourage us. Make your voice heard. Make your ideas heard. It is your right and obligation as a member of the community.

### *Internship Is Critical To Your Development*

It is anticipated that, as an extension to the skills in formal educational settings, government (appropriate agency or authority) would religiously liaise with industry to accept students as interns for the duration of six months or as appropriate. For instance, Businesses and other financial institutions by specifying agreement would accept banking and finance students as interns for training as they would if they were to employ them as their staff and so on for all other industries.

This should take place during vacations as conversely, skills bridging programme kicks in after school.

Already, a number of tertiary institutions have in place well tested internship programmes. It is worth encouraging other institutions to follow a similar course of action. What government can do temporarily is to come in to lend specific support when called upon in critical areas by the institutions involved. Technically, the participating institutions are qualified to handle the programme.

Internship at the Presidency and offices of Ministers are also critical. Interns at the nerve centre of government would train in the art of Diplomacy, Communication, and areas such as Accounting and Management of policy and human resource. This should not be reserved for the youth wings of current governments but for all who are qualified and willing. The Forces should also consider interns.

There are numerous roles to consider for the interns within their ranks. These include engineering, finance, management, administrative works, fabrication works, architecture among others.

### *Churches, Muslims Have Key Roles In Vocational Training*

Churches and Muslim groups have important roles to play in Vocational Training. Churches here include the Pentecostal, Orthodox and the Spiritual ones. The craze has now been to facilitate University Colleges, where obviously there are proven profit margins and psychological edge of importance. The call is for the Houses of God to get involved in poverty alleviation programmes, such as ADRA (Adventist Relief Agency), which benefits the real economy. Thus the need for the Church to get involved in vocational or any related skills based programme would boost the efforts of other stakeholders. Such a venture would do much for the body as much as the unadulterated Gospel of God does for the soul. The Church should take a central role in the vocational education of the youth.

Skills training are closely related to job creation. Per the orientation proposed in this book, those of you without certified skills should not be allowed onto the job market and for that matter, those of you already on the job market without skills should be recalled for training if indeed you are to survive with dignity and make a meaningful contribution to the economy. It is indeed necessary to 'promote flexibility in training systems and collaboration between training institutions and employers' and the Church has the capacity and the calling to be at the centre of such training towards skills acquisition.

It would be a national disgrace and moral flop to allow any section of you on the job market without adequate skills for economic survival. The skills we profess to give them in the vocational institutions should be adequate and appropriate for the job market.

It is an economic as well as moral obligation that the Houses of God assist the society to offer this opportunity to you. It should not be a privilege but a right of every youth of the House of God. An explicit right which the society owes to the youth if we so wish them to be productive citizens.

### Recruitment Centres Are Useful

Recruitment Centres, mainly the private sector led, have become popular among students and white colour job seekers. They play important roles in the location of jobs. Their activeness lifts much burden off the levers of school jobcentres. Without urging for brash government intrusion into their operations, it is important for government to recognise their contributions in the employment placement programmes for the youth. Regulating their activities by way of legislative instrument and compliance code would not be out of place.

Again it is important for governments, through a Ministry or an Authority, to provide assistance in terms of capacity building and liaison with employers.

## *The Focus Of Student Union*

Funding of job fairs should be considered by the government for a period till the recruitment industry is maturing to be on its own. Furthermore, employers should be encouraged to support campus job fairs. On this issue, student leaders and groups should work to bring consultants and business leaders to campuses for the purposes of education.

Often entry to the floor of these fairs to just register and speak to a consultant is at a fee. One of the arguments for this fee is that, the fees go to pay for the organisation and administrative cost. It is fair for business but we should not compound the headaches of the job seekers when speaking to a counsellor does not guarantee automatic job placement. SRCs, National Union of Students, could easily make recruitment drives part of their annual programmes.

Another criticism of recruitment firms is the narrowness of their target market. The long time practice has been to consider University, Polytechnic and Diploma graduates, leaving out graduates from technical and vocational centres. It is important to consider skilled labour such as those in the handicraft and related industries. The case of unskilled labour could also be considered by the Centres for helping hands as labourers. It is envisaged that with the inactivity of labour offices across the country, it would be important for the private sector to also venture in Total Recruitment and fill the vacuum so created by poorly performing labour offices.

## A Job Centre and Privately Owned Recruitment Centre Could Co-Exist

It is important to mention briefly though, that the concept of job centres and the expanded role of recruitment consultancies could co-exist. That is to say, primarily, recruitment centres have their advantages over jobcentres. Recruitment centres follow up on job openings, they have stronger ties with employers and among others, help job seekers in CV preparation and job search techniques. Others offer counselling services.

## Part Time Jobs

Short term job contract and part-time job concepts should be explored by the youth, government and employers. Our traditional view of work has been lifetime jobs. Times have changed and with it the nature of employment. It is something the government in the short term can do little about.

Suffice to say, it is important to alert job seekers to this concept, regardless of growing and harmonising the activities of the informal sector into mainstream to boost opportunities. Part time contract and short term employment hold great potential for employment if properly nurtured.

## Youth Employment Programmes: The Ghana Model

### Brief Overview of the programme

The National Youth Employment Programme (NYEP) in no doubt has lofty promises for the youth. The programme is a straightforward fast track stop gap programme for providing low end jobs for low unskilled youth whilst at the same time, giving them the room for growth and further development.

The programme selected key areas of need (models) and sought to enrol the youth on them. Some of these models included farming, teaching, sanitation, ICT, and road maintenance. The programme was a breather, giving 'students' a two-year period for them to acquire higher skills and move up the ladder.

On the issue of management, the programme has national, regional and district coordinators.

## Comments

The programme has been implemented in a manner to seem like an adventure to keep the youth off the street and not the lofty policy that the youth seem to be advocating for to make them competitive in the 21st century.

Despite the fact that few could question the breadth of the programme, there is much to be done about its depth and how it can migrate the youth into formal training programmes. This would be cost effective in making it sustainable by adjoining it to Technical Institutes instead of making it self-sustaining on its own since it does not have an immediate strong foundation and structures.

Considering the high levels of illiteracy, lack of skills and high unemployment among the youth in many economies, it is important to acknowledge that, the NYEP in its practical form is acceptable and realistic.

Developing the migratory route for you on the programme to pursue progression into higher levels of skills acquisition is critical. That, it is inconceivable for the youth to continue collecting garbage for three (3) years using the same tools and equipment without improvement and migration to the use of higher and better equipment and (or) graduate into better roles as entrepreneurs, and eventual employers in their respective fields.

Until the programme creates and nurtures progression routes, it would be difficult to justify the programme to middle level skills holders. The point is that, if you started as a farmer on the programme using machete and traditional methods, by progression, it is expected that with time, you would learn to become a better farmer by using better farming methods; use of machinery and even learn to market your products outside your village and even beyond to regional markets.

You would also learn to manage your farm in best practices and by so doing improve your life to the eventual growth of the society. The wealth of a society should be judged by the quality of the life of its youth. If there is progression, it is important to dream that, your development would be guaranteed and with it, a dream of a better and more prosperous future.

## Challenges facing The Programme

The pragmatic programme is not without self-created challenges, mainly political. Opportunism and low mindedness among some politicians have mostly taken broad based support from the programme. Many proposals could be put forward for the improvement of the programme. It is my firm belief that, the first challenge is to wrestle the programme from direct political control.

In this line, appointment of national coordinators should be devoid of political influence, even in its latent form. Thus, the appointment of the managers of the programme at all levels should be subject to the Civil Services Commission and not by political appointment.

The programme has not been followed up by the necessary support to prepare the youth to go beyond the first stage. That is to say, the stop gap role of giving the youth temporal employment as they seek permanent employment through the acquisition of skills and further learning has rather become a mirage.

The graduation period was supposed to be two years. This was poorly communicated or the most tedious job of training, coaching and (or) counselling the 'employees' to further-up was not done. So the youth took it as a 'job' for life and did not further-up. For instance, many of those who were employed in the classroom neither improved their grades to qualify for teacher training colleges nor looked for other avenues of self development.

Garbage collectors, for two years now have been performing the same task without value. So are the would-be 'mechanised farmers' and street cleaners.

The implementers and managers of the programme took their eyes off the ball as soon as the programme left the headline and won wide political support. Since the youth on the programme have not benefited from new training and resources to enable them survive on their own, it is important not to wean them off the programme. Government should extend their stay on the programme. But as quickly as possible, government should forcefully push for their absorption into the real world with best and more employable skills through training.

## A Positive Intervention

Without doubt, the national youth employment programme has contributed to the creation of temporal employment for thousands of youth who otherwise would have ended up in dire circumstances. The programme further prevented a youth implosion which was past the budding stage.

The programme is a positive intervention which has taken many a youth out of crime ways. Without it, it is hard to imagine the fate of thousands of youth on the programme. Nevertheless, the programme has flaws and challenges which need to be addressed urgently.

Perhaps the single riskiest challenge to the programme is corruption.

## Public Works Projects — Senegal

(Source: Sarr, M. (2000). Youth Employment in Africa: The Senegalese Experience, )

*Agence d' Exécution des Travaux d' Intérêt Public (AGETIP) was launched in 1989 by the government of Senegal, with the support of the World Bank and the African Development Bank, to provide short-term employment to a growing number of un-employed youth.*

*The central mandate of the programme was to sub-contract, coordinate and supervise the execution of construction, reha-bilitation, and maintenance of urban infrastructure and to fa-cilitate the provision of essential services. During the first four-*

*year phase, AGETIP enabled the creation of about 80,000 jobs by subcontracting 416 components of public works projects to small-scale entrepreneurs.*

*Largely addressing urban issues such as the deterioration of infrastructure, mounting social unrest and under-employment, AGETIP quickly expanded to over 3,200 projects contributing to the creation of 350,000 short-term jobs annually and 6000 permanent positions. Similar programmes have been launched in Burkina Faso, Benin, Chad, Togo, Madagascar, Mali, Mauritania, and Niger with the support of their development partners.*

# 13

## Youth Entrepreneurship, Apprenticeship and Volunteerism

*'Nobody talks about entrepreneurship as survival, but that's exactly what it is and what nurtures creative thinking.'*

Anita Roddick, DBE (23rd October 1942 – 10th September 2007) Founder of The Body Shop

## Essence of the Concept

The concept of entrepreneurship is useful in creating self-employment. For others, entrepreneurship is a route to fulfilment. It nurtures survival instincts and has given birth to fulfilment in the lives of many successful people. It gives ample space for dreamers to challenge the business status quo and create their own world. There are a few of you who are tough, skilled, and resourceful enough to create your own businesses.

The need for policy is to ensure that, all classes of youth are introduced to the culture of entrepreneurship. With jobs hard to come by, as many of you as possible should be supported to successfully set up your own businesses.

In the manner of establishing a platform for the youth in this direction, four (4) institutions are required to work in concert:

1.  A National Board for Small Scale Industries (to provide technical direction and guidelines)

2.  National Incubation Centres (to provide space and day to day technical advice)

3.  A Bank For Small Scale Businesses (to provide financial facilities and loan guarantees)

4.  A Venture Capital Fund ( to provide funding for start-ups)

The National Youth Authority or an appropriate institution and the National Board for Small Scale Industries should work together to establish training models for those of you wishing to start your own businesses or to grow your businesses.

Private option could be pursued. In this direction, governments should encourage private centres to undertake seminars, courses in entrepreneurship and office space for some of the younger start-ups on commercial basis. Governments can set up mentoring and training or business proposal writing programmes for youth entrepreneurs with a special focus on helping you set-up your own businesses and helping the same to grow them. Another option is to add entrepreneurial courses to NVTIs, STEPs and in universities and secondary schools.

## A National Mentoring Programme

In Ghana, Joy FM, a leading private radio station, has started a programme by matching some of you with business leaders and established entrepreneurs. Similar programmes on a more diverse and larger scale could be supported by government and the private sector to provide real life skills to you.

In pursuit of sustaining entrepreneurship, it is important to ensure that funding and technical advice are available to you. This funding could be from government or private sources. Regardless of the sources of the funding, it should be affordable, with low interest rates. Grants would be the best source for you. But with the involvement of the private sector, this option is most unlikely.

Furthermore, these loans should have long term repayable terms.

## Business Incubation Centres

One critical programme which could provide substantive and long term services to the youth should centre on incubation centres. Traditionally, incubation centres give office space and technical advice in the early years of start-ups with the capacity, by design, to support any area of entrepreneurial direction government policies indicate.

There should be the need for direct government intervention in the setting up of structures to support you. For many reasons, government has not warmed up adequately to the concept of incubation centres.

In this light, three (3) options could be pursued by government:

1. Fully government funded programme

2. Private sector owned programme with incentives such as loan guarantees, tax rebates from the government

3. Government-private sector ownership

The tested philosophical underpinning here is that, you need a platform and protection in your early entrepreneurial life, without which you would be unable to survive on your own. In extending this assistance, the government and partners would create a nest where young entrepreneurs would be protected for a reasonable period of time. Bearing in mind that, monetary assistance would not necessarily be enough to guarantee your success.

### *Entrepreneurship Requires Skills*

The high level of expertise required to successfully manage a business, coupled with the cost of rent, makes it necessary for the government, either singularly or in partnership, to support the culture of the business incubation centres. These incubation centres should be established with the core goal of providing the necessary technical support and protection for young entrepreneurs during the critical early stages of their businesses.

It is worth noting that, certain key programmes such as youth entrepreneurship competition would harness interest in entrepreneurship and business creation among you. This would involve business plan competition, proposals and business concepts competition. These should be at the District, Regional and National levels or a progression from the District to the National levels. It could also be on the basis of categories, say, in ICT, farming, Services or any other field with a high level of success. Various categories could be added.

The first, say, ten from each category would receive prizes not only in monetary forms but in other forms such as equipments, technical advice packages, space at incubation centres and in other forms. The National Board for Small Scale Industries, in collaboration with the Ministry Of Trade and Industry and National Youth Authority would supervise and manage winning projects till they are matured to be on their own.

## *Three Categories Of Entrepreneurs To Be Created*

As a matter of national priority, three categories of entrepreneurs should be encouraged across all sectors of commerce. Programmes should be deliberate to aggregate youth entrepreneurs into:

1. Community-based Entrepreneurs
2. National Entrepreneurs
3. Global Entrepreneurs

## Community-based Entrepreneurs

Community-based entrepreneurs are those who trade within one particular town, village or city. Their operations centre within one of these units only, and without any immediate intention to expand into another village, town or city.

## National Entrepreneurs

The second class are those trained to have the capacity to trade on a nationwide basis.

## Global Entrepreneurs

The third are those who would build the capacity and ambition to trade in international markets. They should be assisted to build the network to make international contacts to be on their own in manufacturing and export facilitations. Thus, this class is those of you who would be able to build businesses and expand them to the international markets. There should be deliberate efforts in selecting youth entrepreneurs into these categories.

Of these, much resource should be spent on the latter two. They have the bigger opportunities and higher returns.

## Apprenticeship

The 2007 Education Reform Committee, Ghana, headed by Professor Anamoah-Mensah, made insightful recommendations on the issue of apprenticeship underlining its eminent role in national development. It recommends that the State should:

1. Constitute a National Apprentice Training Board, among other things to oversee and regulate apprentice training and handle issues concerning registration, content, duration and certification.

2. Formalise Community-Based Apprentice Training Schemes in all districts to cater for the youth.

3. Supporting institutions such as Regional Technology Transfer Centres (RTTCs), and Ghana Regional Appropriate Technology Industrial Service (GRATIS), ICCES, Opportunities Industrialisation Centres (OIC), youth leadership institutes, the private sector and other organisations including NGOs to increase capacity and expand their coverage and enrolment of apprentice.

The issue of apprenticeship has been an already popular concept in our communities. What is being advocated for is for the government through the National Apprenticeship Training Board (NATB) under the National Youth Authority (NYA), to take a meaningful central role and assume leadership in apprenticeship training programmes. The NYA or NATB with the necessary legislative mandate, capacity, and resources, should not only register the youth but also create an inventory of all informal training centres, among which are carpenters, tailors, seamstresses, fabricators, masons, bakers, and other skill areas as the NATB may identify.

This inventory is critical in establishing a strong basis for effective management, offer of support and guard against corruption. The NYA should certify privately registered centres, under laid down standards to train the youth in their respective fields.

## The Issue Of Funding

Government should bear the administrative cost of managing the centres through the National Youth Authority (NYA). This notwithstanding, you should be motivated to patronise the programme and further get the society behind the programme. There would be the need for effective data collection and management of the centres. It is also necessary to ensure community and (or) District ownership. It is also important to make the programme District Based.

The district-managed training programme would be appropriate for the benefit of stronger supervision and cost effectiveness. The National Youth Authority (NYA) would continue to perform its coordination, training, registration, content development and course duration and certification roles. It should also be responsible for supervising various Districts with respect to this programme.

The question of 'Who funds the apprenticeship training?' is critical to the sustainability of the programme. The question of 'How do we monitor, so that the system is not abused?' requires further consideration.

The cost of the programme comes from three main sources. First, the administrative cost from both the NYA and NATB at the District level. Second is the cost to apprenticeship centres and thirdly, the cost of acquiring learning tools, building workshops and support allowance for the trainees. Government funding for allowances would have lifted a heavy burden off the shoulders of parents and the youth, who largely have grown to support themselves. This is unrealistic considering the huge management cost and management challenges the board is likely to face.

It is important for governments to foot the administrative and tuition costs of the programme as stated earlier. If accurate data are available, District Assemblies or relevant bodies should give loan guarantees for the cost of tools and machinery for certified graduates of the apprenticeship programme.

The question of working space after graduation is also critical. National incubation centres would not be appropriate for graduates of the system. This is partly due to the diverse and remote centres the apprenticeship programme is to run. Even in situations where it would be possible for apprentice to have access to incubation centres, it is foreseen that centres would not produce enough space for graduates.

## Is A Partnership Required?

In order to foster synergy and share risks, partnerships should be encouraged among graduates for you to work together under 'common-roof' after graduation. Thus, graduates are advised to work together under one facility. Each worker retains his earnings and customers. Indeed, each worker is independent of other workers with the exception of their working space.

The 'common-roof' policy is necessary for ensuring better supervision, provision of technical advice, and monitoring. It also reduces the burden of acquiring workshops which would be expensive for individuals. Those of you unable to be awarded working spaces at the incubation centres would be advised to take this option.

Community ownership and supervision would be important measures in sustaining the programme. It is imperative

174

to consider measures to curtail such abuses as bloating of apprentice register, number of training centres and related expenditure. Thus, communities should take the programme as their bona fide product. Communities could even construct the workshops for apprentice to use the space at a fee.

## *The Physically Challenged*

There ought to be a separate programme for the physically challenged in the society. The programme for the disabled should be handled by the Communities. This is due to the dispersed and unregulated nature of rural settlements. For the government to centrally manage the programme is to ask for huge unsustainable financial burden. Government can provide technical advice in the planning, implementation and management of the respective programmes. But the supervisory roles at centres should be left to the District assemblies and the respective communities.

# 14

## Delinquency and Drugs: The Roles of Stakeholders

*'Drug addiction destroys lives, tears families apart and harms society.'*

Unknown

## *The Riyadh Guidelines*

The Riyadh guidelines offers sound basis and principles for the containment of youth delinquency within the boundaries of national and international laws. Thus, offering a framework of broad consensus with the aim of instituting a fair, common and avoidance of discrimination against sections of the youth, especially those from volatile and vulnerable communities. Irrespective of the ideological position of political leadership on the causes of juvenile delinquency, popular opinion and the capacity of civil society groups, it is necessary to acknowledge that the delinquent youth has a right to education and reformation as much as any other youth in the society.

As a result of the huge cost of crime, it is necessary to ensure that every delinquent is accorded the right opportunity, largely at the expense of the State, to help them reform and acquire the necessary will to fight delinquent behaviours and contribute to national development.

In the fight against juvenile delinquency, it requires 'efforts on the part of the entire society to ensure the harmonious development of adolescents, with respect for and promotion of their personality from early childhood'. This is a fact.

There is a strong voice among psychologist that, 'young persons should have an active role and partnership within society and should not be considered as mere objects of socialization or control'. By involving them, the argument is that they would identify themselves as part of the society, whilst within the same space, we build in them, the concepts of self-belief and belongingness.

Community-based 'services and programmes should be developed for the prevention of juvenile delinquency, particularly where no agencies have yet been established'. Thus, various communities within national laws should take concrete steps in addressing juvenile delinquency rather than leaving it to central governments alone.

## Traditional Fight against Juvenile Delinquency

It is widely agreed among experts that, 'young people constitute one of the most criminally active segments of the population.' These behaviours are not only about violent crime, petty robbery, rioting, drug and substance abuse, but in addition, truancy and anti-social behaviour.

Among many societies, it is believed that, 'their intensity and gravity depend mostly on the social, economic and cultural conditions in each country'. However, 'an apparent world-wide increase in juvenile criminality combined with economic recession, especially in marginal sectors of urban centres', gives enormous cause for concern.

Repeated youth crime has become a major concern to government and society. This concern is worth a great deal of attention considering the potential contribution of youth to national development and, the cost of crime to society.

As policy makers and society brood over for lasting solutions, it is prudent to ensure that, in the immediate term, youth of all ages, background and traditions are given the necessary assistance needed to help those caught in the web. Furthermore, considering that, the delinquent youth has the propensity to grow into a hardened adult criminal, it is important to urge society to make serious efforts in the fight to redeem our most abundant and cherished resource: our youth.

Traditionally, theoretical causes which have been assigned to juvenile delinquency include 'rational cause, social disorganization, strain, differential association and labeling and male phenomenon'. Suffice to say, models based upon these views are still valid, bearing limited appraisal to make them more relevant to the needs of the times and each society.

On one hand, a school of thought (Rational choice) posits that, causes of juvenile delinquency and crime lie within the individual rather than his external environment. For believers in this theory, 'offenders are motivated by rational self-interest', and the importance of free will and personal responsibility is emphasised.

Thus, proponents believe and attribute 'variation in crime and delinquency over time and among territories to the absence of or breakdown of communal institutions (e.g. family, school, Church and local government) and communal relationships that traditionally encouraged cooperative relationships among people'.

Additionally, theorists who believe in the 'strain theory', associated with the work of Robert Merton hold that, 'There are institutionalized paths to success in society.' Thus, once these paths are created and followed, there would be a realistic likelihood of success in fighting youth crime and delinquency. In this light, to fight juvenile delinquency is to create opportunities for the youth to achieve their aspirations. Thus these opportunities would enlighten the youth that, following anti social characters would only make their dream of a better future elusive.

This opinion is further reinforced by the position that, 'Crime is caused by the difficulty those in poverty have in achieving socially valued goals by legitimate means.' The theory is that, those with, for instance, poor educational attainment have difficulty in achieving wealth and status by securing well paid employment, thus they are more likely to use criminal means to obtain these goals.

This position is problematic. There are young persons from affluent neighbourhoods and families who have turned out to be delinquents. Perhaps the difference is the magnitude. The common belief though, perhaps rightly so, is that the crime rate in the ghettoes and low income areas are higher.

In this light, Merton suggests five adaptations young people adopt in such situations. These are 'innovation, retreatism, ritualism, conformity and rebellion.' Merton defined his innovative individuals as those 'who accept socially approved goals, but not necessarily the socially approved means.' On the other hand, he referred to retreatism as 'those who reject socially approved goals and the means for acquiring them'. Ritualism denotes 'those who buy into a system of socially approved means, but lose sight of the goals.' Merton believed that 'drug users are in this category.' Those who conform to the system's means and goals' Merton categorized them to conformity. Accordingly, there are those who create their own paths by negating 'socially approved goals and means by creating a new system of acceptable goals and means'. He referred to these as the rebellious.

A difficulty with strain theory is that, 'it does not explore why children of low-income families would have poor educational attainment in the first place. More importantly is the fact that, much youth crime does not have an economic motivation. Strain theory also fails to explain violent crime, the type of youth crime which causes the most anxiety to the public'.

Differential association has been part of the mainstream positions on juvenile delinquency and incidents of violent crime. Basically, it considers the influence of group associations, peer pressure and how 'the existence of gangs could lead them into crime'. It stresses that, 'Young people are motivated to commit crimes by delinquent peers, and learn criminal skills from them.'

There is no doubt that, young people are adventurous, curious and sometimes bold beyond reason. It is important to guide their minds to make sure that they are not overly exposed. This is not to advocate for censorship or any overt restrictions. The argument is for parents, society and any party to youth development to consider the nature of the modern generation of young persons in their designs and overtures.

Another school of thought holds it that, 'Once young people have been labelled as criminal, they are more likely to offend.' The idea is that 'once labelled as a deviant, a young person may accept that role, and be more likely to associate with others who have been similarly labelled'. Other authors point out that, 'male children from poor families are more likely to be labelled deviant.'

Many feminist academics hold the view that, 'Youth crime is disproportionately committed by young men.' One of such explanation is that, 'masculinity may make young men more likely to offend.' That being tough, powerful, aggressive, daring and competitive may be a way young men attempt to express their masculinity.' The argument here is that, for male young persons to portray these qualities as society expects of them, they are 'more likely to engage in antisocial and criminal behaviour.'

Biological reasons have also been attributed to male vulnerability to crime. Thus 'adolescent males who possess a certain type of variation in a specific gene are more likely to flock to delinquent peers'. This position was published in the Journal of Genetic Psychology in late 2008. The authenticity of such academic positions is never in doubt.

The thrust of thought here is to establish a pattern that, the issue of juvenile delinquency is a deeply considered issue among intellectuals and thus, it goes beyond the mere statements of 'locate and quote' politicians, floating Non- Governmental Organisations and opportunists.

## Beyond the Academics and Theories

Beyond the tortuous mental alienations of theories and statistics lies the reality that juvenile crime is robbing society of financial resources and talents. As such, urgent and coordinated efforts on the part of policy makers, governments, the clergy, the mass media and traditional society are needed to contain the situation.

We owe it to our youth, and the future of Africa to exert energies in positioning our youth to benefit from the best this century offers. We are living in wonderful times in terms of promise. Education is no longer a privilege. Neither is the information the preserve of the few. Every corner of our urban centres offers opportunities to socialize, surf the net, learn and do so many things hitherto not available to a generation few years ago. Telecommunication in many of its various forms is affordable. Television and radio are affordable by many. We need to help delinquents to reform and join in sharing in the opportunities in the society.

## Risks Factors

### Individual Risk Factors

Some psychologists hold the position that, 'Individual psychological or behavioural risk factors that may make offending more likely include intelligence, impulsiveness or the inability to delay gratification, aggression, empathy, and restlessness.'

Accordingly, they argue that, 'Children with low intelligence are likely to do worse in school' and as a result 'may increase the chances of offending because of low educational attainment, low attachment in school, and low educational aspirations. These are all risk factors for offending in themselves.'

It is a widely held view, although with little scientific support, that, 'Children who perform poorly at school are also more likely to be truants.' Perhaps, rightly, truant young people are more likely to be offending.

## Family Environment

There is no doubt that, the African family environment has important roles to play in the life of the youth. Family as used here includes the immediate and extended families. Our societies continue to trust so much to the family in the life of the young. These include guidance, education on matters of society, tradition and values. More particularly, the role of the family had included the way young people are brought up.

It is established that, 'children brought up by lone parents are more likely to start offending than those who live with two natural parents.' However, the attachment a child feels towards their parent(s) and the level of parental supervision should be taken into account.

It is observed that, children in single parent families are no more likely to offend than others.' When parents 'commonly do not know where their children are, what their activities are, or who their friends are, children are more likely to be truants and have delinquent friends, each of which is linked to offending'. Without parents having a direct idea of what their children are reading or picking up from friends and the various sources of knowledge, it would be difficult to educate and guide them.

## Proposals

### *The Family: Nuclear and Extended*

The family is an important stakeholder in the formation of the youth. The family is a pillar standing tall behind the parent and the youth. The family provides support for the parents as well. In our traditional society, young persons are as much a child of the family as they are to their parents. Under this code, any member of the family could imbue knowledge and wisdom, and correct a wayward youth.

The control of any member of the family on the youth was as strong as the parent could have. After all, the youth is a child of the family and for the society; a 'son', who would one day uphold the honour, dignity and name of the family. His conduct within or outside the community reflected the family first and parents second.

Despite the fact that the current time has brought in its wake some level of changes, this has not and should not be left to affect the role of the family in the life of the youth. First, let's observe that, it is incumbent upon families to reassert their traditional roles in the lives of the youth. That is to say, the provision of material and moral support, coaching and counselling of the youth, should rather be intensified and not otherwise. Families should begin the traditional (nuclear and extended) meetings, where the youth and other members are advised on the ways of life, rebuked for wrong acts and congratulated for good deeds.

The nuclear family of our modern era should begin to retrace the steps back to the larger family. We are one and economic factors and 'modernity' should not be allowed to dictate the direction of our families. This is not to disregard the fact that, many family members have turned family ties into an economic burden.

By allowing the dissociation of the nuclear family from the extended family, we allow the disintegration of our society. In the course of this action, we have allowed the basic essence of our society to be threatened by external abrasive cultures and failed value systems.

Thus we have lost essential values which formed the basis of our society. Sharing, generosity, honesty, tolerance, respect for life and dignity are all threatened in the process. As such, the disintegration of these bonds has given way to greed, self-centeredness, material craze and hatred. Part of the results is an extremely volatile and wayward youth.

There is nothing stopping any society from embracing the inherent positive values in the tradition of the extended family system whilst in another breadth refining and (or) diminishing the burdensome aspect of it. The extended family was a blessing to every family until some of us became beggars, lazy and others selfish and mean. This minor aberration should in no way be allowed to negate the enormous assets of the extended family.

As it is expected, the youth ought to see beyond his father and mother and embrace the other members of the family, rich or poor. In like manner, every youth and members of the family must endeavour to be his own man, carrying his own burden.

It is important to urge that, parents should learn about youth development in the manner that modern times demand. Parents ought to appreciate the orientations of the youth in matters of education, career choices, value systems and their aspirations. This should be done largely through regular dialogue and family meetings.

There should be a public education to keep parents and family in tune with the lines of thinking and current trends in youth behaviour and influencing factors. The nature of the youth has changed and it is important that parents keep abreast with them. In this light, this objective could be achieved through advocacy, drama, radio education and community debates. Each family should share knowledge and values unlimitedly.

## Family Welfare Systems

By family welfare system, the idea is that, families should create a fund to support the education, apprenticeship, business start-up or expansion and any other relevant venture the youth (member of the family) may seek to enter. In certain families, the amounts given are in a form of grants. In others, they are payable with interest over a year. Some families also do not charge an interest rate. The amount borrowed is paid back as it was given.

In many instances, well-to-do members of the family offer assistance or accommodation as the case may require. For example, young members of the family who may wish to learn a trade in the big towns would be offered accommodation or helped to secure one by members of the family who are resident in the respective towns or have the means to assist. Such actions were seen as a service to family rather than an act of heroism commanding mountains of adulation.

A point here is that, this welfare system should not be left with only government which is in no position to sustain such a system. It is the pride of the family to take care of her own members.

The family should be a friend, father and mother to the youth. And the more the family takes control of the moral and spiritual needs of the youth, there is hope that, most of the problems of the lost generations should not be made to repeat today. It is worth noting that, this role, if effectively done, would correct many of the acts which unknowingly trap the youth.

The family's vigilance might not be enough to contain those already in the net of social crimes and drugs. These classes of the youth would need professional advice and the support of stakeholders such as the Church, Civil Society, the Mass Media, the Department of Corrections and Social Welfare.

Nevertheless, it is important for the family to get involved in the correction of their children. Their involvement could be passive or active. In this sense, passive participation is where the parents observe the counselling processes and give indirect support to counsellors. In active participation, parents take part in the counselling processes at the behest of professional counsellors. This method should be open to parents who have some level of training in youth counselling.

Largely, parents should be passive observers. Once the youth show signs of delinquency, parents would need professional support. Another role parents should play is the provision of information about their children's behaviour, associations, and other observable changes in their social life patterns. If delinquent behaviours are observed early, remedies could be offered to the youth than to let them turn into hardened criminals and deviants.

## Families as Watchdogs

The family should be a watchdog over parents. This statement is made specific to our traditional values, by which, the youth becomes the responsibility of the family, the parents and by extension, the whole society. The interconnection among the youth, family and the society calls for policies to involve these three, bearing in mind their closeness and inseparability in our societies. It is for this reason that the breakdown of each of these units should be of concern to policy makers and the society.

The unbreakable chain joining the youth, family and the society should motivate our willingness to create a better, prosperous and strong society. On this, each stakeholder should be supported, urged or criticized to perform its role adequately.

A question then arises out of this position of promoting a unified three-pronged policy. What happens to the policy should a unit fall behind? Such a situation would mean that, the failure of that unit would pull the others down. Disaggregating the units then would be a better option. Nevertheless, managers of the various units could through established protocols secure cordial working relationships by which ideas and knowledge bank could be built and shared without necessarily resorting to a policy document to ensure the coordination among the players. In this light, family counselling is critical.

It is important to mention that, the distinction between the immediate and extended family is important at this point. This distinction is important as a result of the various roles of each unit. The immediate family is the first line of education. Parents groom their children in a manner consistent with the values of the society and future aspirations. The family could deal with the early challenges of the youth. On an occasion when the youth becomes much of a burden for the family, the extended family through the family head or an elder would rise up and assist or take up the responsibility. The family should not leave the youth to the central government or social workers. Even though the youth is largely considered the asset of the nation, it is important to observe that, they are the pride and the standard bearer of the family.

In reconstituting the family concept, there are key stakeholders to consider. These should include the media, society and chieftaincy. These institutions are critical in forging strong alliances towards the attainment of a strong pillar for the youth: a stable family.

## Traditional Mass Media

The media—with its reach, the ability to set agenda, and its 'god' status in the eyes of the masses—should attempt to educate the youth on family values to the society. Debates could be generated on the essence of the family unit among others to psyche society up by highlighting the inherent beauty of the family system. Thus the media, if they set the agenda, should guide and sustain the same for the purpose of inspiring a broken society to adhere to a key pillar of our society, the family unit. This should as much as possible be treated by the mass media as more of a social duty rather than a commercial one, because no stakeholder in the society could afford a whole generation of wayward, irritant youth.

A young person without a root, vision, sense of direction and belongingness is a threat to himself and his society. Likewise a generation without purpose and direction.

## Chieftaincy Institution

Chieftaincy, having made many unsavoury headlines in recent years, perhaps from a humble point of view, the time has come for this pivotal institution to reassert its custodial duties to the youth and society. There should be a deliberate crusade to achieve this goal.

The proposition here is not the cosmetic media stunts which have become prevalent. This is a call for grass root education, where chiefs and sub-chiefs would engage their societies in meaningful 'Nim-tree' and Baobab-tree discussions to establish codes and reinstate the position of the family in the society and more importantly to the youth.

It is worth noting that, this cannot be achieved by a legislative outburst. Thus, beyond facility and funding, politicians should take a low profile. It is worth noting that, no single political party should claim ownership of any such crusade. Rather, all political parties should see themselves as contributors of a struggle, which may outlive their terms of temporal political office.

Another area the government should intervene is the design of programmes through its Social Services Programme. In countries where Social Services Commission is virtually on its knees, a National Commission on Culture or any other body appropriate should be the coordinating body to serve as cement among the various stakeholders in this endeavour.

Another leader in this case should be the National House of Chiefs or any relevant central traditional authority. Beyond the central body taking the lead, various community chiefs and leaders should endeavour to take their own initiatives towards the goal.

### The World Wide Web: Internet

The youth of today face more challenges in their life choices than a decade or two ago. The advent of technology, mass media, and the pursuit of profits by the corporate bodies have invaded their delicate shells with carefully and subtly packaged items which only see them as fresh markets target rather than national assets to be nurtured and groomed.

The media instruments are, by and large, important tools in national development but their downside has been devastating. More so, when state institutions are largely redundant or poorly equipped to act in a manner which would offset the negative lures of the cheap information and youth targeting by the corporate profiteering world.

Despite the fact that censorship of the media does not make commercial sense, it is important for consideration to be made in finding proactive means of checking the media and corporate business from targeting the youth. The movie industry with their daring near explicit sex scenes and glorification of crime and violence should be dealt with in a manner that would not hurt or curtail the growth of the industry.

The World Wide Web (the internet) is the worst culprit. Free Movie software enables the youth to download and watch all sorts of movies and materials at relatively cheap cost. This is a challenge internet cafés could help, albeit, minimally. Currently, most mobile carriers provide internet access on their networks. This is an important feature to enable subscribers access their mail on the go.

In this light, mobile carriers should be in a position to block internet porn sites and other contents which are at variance with our values to phones registered to the underage. In this vein, birth certificates and parent consent notes could be sought from underage young people. As a result, there should be a real time periodic review of registration data due to growth of underage holders. In the case of Ghana, with registration age pegged at eighteen (18) years, the Mobile carriers have no legal right to block any subscriber from accessing any internet site unless it is explicitly registered to a minor. The assumption is that all subscribers are legal. Under this issue, parents should be the first guards.

## *The Roles of the Community*

Society and its neighbourhoods play an important role in delinquency and youth crimes. Every society has its value systems. It is important to note that, the society, family and neighbourhood have to coordinate their efforts to ensure that, we achieve our aim of near zero delinquency and drift among the youth in the community. In this vein, there should be enhanced collaborative responsibilities among the various active players.

The community should adopt the youth as her children and commit necessary resources to their development for the sustainability and development of the society. To this end, it is worth suggesting that, the concept of youth mentoring should be encouraged at the community level.

The practicality of the concepts should rest on role modelling where the society would highlight the achievements of prominent citizens. It may go like telling the youth that, 'You can be or be greater than him.'

Furthermore, these role models should live morally upright lives to inspire the youth. The selection of these role models should be carefully done. We do not want a situation where role models would turn out later to be crooks and bad characters.

It is necessary for the community to get directly involved in fighting delinquency considering the number of challenges facing the youth: the lack of resources to sustain large programmes, lack of adequate social workers and weaknesses in the Department of Social Welfare, apathy on the part of the media and civil society's arms length approach to the question of delinquency and drug abuse are key challenges.

Dissemination of information by Information Services, Mass Media and Traditional means like the gong-gong should be encouraged unequivocally. The availability of services, opportunities in the society for the youth should be the centre of such information to ensure the youth have a clear idea of services available and where to access them. It is worth stating that, 'the mass media generally, and the television and film media in particular, should be encouraged to minimize the level of pornography, drugs and violence'. Furthermore, 'the media should portray them in bad light as well as avoid demeaning and degrading presentations, especially of children, women, interpersonal relations, and to promote egalitarian principles and roles'.

## The Houses Of God

The Church has important roles in the lives of the youth. It is not enough to preach the gospel, pray and offer occasional advice. This call is for the Church to institutionalise counselling and training programmes for the youth. First, it is important for the Church to consolidate the youth already in the Church and secondly, to reach out to those on the street. The youth who are under the trap of drugs, hopelessness, poverty, hunger and homelessness need the guidance of the Church to point the way to spiritual development. It is important for the Church to use their counselling and financial resources to serve the society's youth bearing in mind that, the 'youth is our best resource' for a secured future of the society and the Church as well.

In this regard, I propose some simple provisions here for the consideration of the Church of our LORD/Religious Groups:

1. Creating an Internal Fund for the rehabilitation of street youth.

2. Constituting a committee for proposing ideas and guidelines for the management of such funds.

3. Churches should institute Youth Outreach Programmes (YOPs) geared towards advancement of the youth. This should cater for both those inside and outside the Church.

4. Churches should also strengthen counselling services for the youth on life choices and career aspirations. Such programmes should be community based and targeted at the vulnerable youth.

5. As part of community service, Churches could build temporary hostel facilities to help shelter the homeless youth or encourage adoption or care parenthood. Under this programme, Church members who could afford to provide food on a regular basis to the hungry could offer those services through the Church. Those with spare rooms could make them available.

On a more elaborate manner, the Church could establish homes for the youth who are homeless and (or) destitute. These centres should not only give shelter and food but training opportunities as well. This training advocated here could be apprenticeship in any relevant skill-based trade the Church may deem fit and can afford. This should not be another academic institute. It should simply be a training centre in programmes such as basketry, carpentry, embroidery, weaving among others. Christ would equally be happy as with winning their souls. This should be done within the law by seeking approval and appropriate accreditation from the relevant Institutions.

The centre should be for the purpose of providing a service and not as a profiteering venture. Already in Ghana, The Presbyterian Church and the Seventh Day Adventists (SDA) have such facilities, giving assistance to the youth. This is commendable.

6. It would be prudent to liaise with the prison services and (or) the department of corrections to institute prison youth services. The emphasis here is not the usual visits to the prisons. The call here is for a professional programme to challenge the status quo and commit resources to delinquents in juvenile correctional facilities for them to acquire basic skills which existing correctional institutions are unable to provide so that, they come out as better persons, focused, confident and skilled in a trade.

7. Advocacy is another area the Church could concentrate on in order to influence policy and the distribution of resources. In this effort, it would be practical for the Church to meet the representatives of the youth, social groups, student leaders, NGOs concerned with

youth welfare, policy makers and technocrats and make proposals with respect to the welfare of young persons or any other area connected with them.

## Slums and Ghettoes

One other important issue worth mentioning, if even in passing, is the slur of ghettoes. Ghettoes have been known to provide safe havens for criminals and traps for the vulnerable youth especially the homeless, poverty stricken and those from hot spots. Ghettoes do not only provide fertile grounds for criminals, they also provide them with the opportunity to recruit vulnerable youth to their fold. The latter action has largely been overlooked in traditional considerations but considering the important role of the youth in development, it is important that District Assemblies and Community leaders fight against ghettoes.

It should be a matter of national priority to clamp down on them. One way of making ghettoes unpopular is to provide opportunities for the youth to train and acquire skills to make them productive to themselves and the larger society.

It is important to clamp down on ghettoes and make them unpopular but above all, the society ought to ascertain the aspirations of the youth and provide opportunities for them to meet these aspirations. The society should help them develop a sense of purpose with the hope that, their aspirations are achievable within their communities and that, the lures of ghettoes are but ephemeral with lifelong destructive consequences.

## *The Role of Community and Student Youth Leaders*

The role of community youth leaders and student leadership is critical in whatever programme enacted to check the lure of ghettoes. Youth leadership as used here refers to youth groups in localities and neighbourhoods.

It is important for society and local authorities to provide opportunities for youth leadership to develop their capabilities. This is important in ensuring that, they acquire the requisite knowledge and capacity to appreciate the challenges facing them. Youth leaders should propose solutions to address the slur of ghettoes and further take part in actual programme of activities in achieving set goals.

The opportunities could be in the form of training, funding of community youth programmes and their direct involvement in policy and programme implementation at the community level. Youth leaders must organize programmes within communities to educate and offer suggestions for helping those already in the snare. Programmes must be practical, relevant and participatory. The community must be involved in the planning, execution and all post-programme activities. The community must see the programmes as their own and that, their success is for their own good.

It is important to state that, youth leadership has a responsibility to show maturity and discipline in their endeavours in order to attract the seriousness required to secure them the necessary resources required for their thrive.

# 15

## Implementing Institution

*'The only justifiable purpose of political institutions is to ensure the unhindered development of the individual'*

Albert Einstein

## Policies Have No Legs

There is no doubt that, policies have no legs to walk on into reality. The traditional track for their movement into reality is through programmes deliberately designed and religiously adhered to. On the other hand, programmes are implemented by institutions. Thus the stronger, effective and resourceful the institution is, the better the programmes are implemented and consequently the effectiveness of the policy in the lives of the intended target.

As such, a National Youth Authority (NYA) should constitute an annual or periodic assembly of stakeholders including youth (activists, student leadership, section of students), policy makers, educationists, counsellors, the clergy and others as the circumstance may allow, to draft a new youth policy or review an existing policy or both, with particular emphasis on skills acquisition, retraining, juvenile correction, national orientation and response to emerging issues. This should be in line with patriotism, independence of thought, internationalization of ideas, youth involvement and participation in the social life of the society and national development.

There should be a clear definition of the progressive roles of the NYA with a clear agenda, timelines, powers and deliverables. The Authority should be supported with adequate resources to be able to meet its obligations.

The NYA should be resourced to perform its functions favourably without political manipulations. As such, the Authority should be independent. It must have right over its policy direction, programmes, hiring of personnel, and its budget (charged onto a skills development levy).

There should be wide ranging consultation with traditional leaders and interest groups outside the youth bracket, as well as with those whose specialty falls outside youth activities. This would ensure the accumulation of knowledge, sharing of experiences and thereby giving the authority impetus and broad base appeal.

The objects of a National Youth Authority (NYA) could further include

1. To co-ordinate all activities, develop and manage an integrated national youth policy;

2. To develop a series of programmes to implement the national youth policy by utilising available resources and expertise. These programmes should be integrated into the vision programme or any other consolidated national development policy;

3. To develop open principles and guidelines and make recommendations to the government for support regarding such principles and guidelines, for future development and implementation of any existing national youth policy;

4. To co-ordinate, direct and monitor the implementation of such principles and guidelines as a matter of priority to national development;

5. To implement measures to address any imbalance, existing or anticipated, relating to the various forms of disadvantaged youth groups or categories.

6. To ensure the synchronisation of approaches by all

organs of state, including districts and provincial administrations, to matters relating to or involving the youth;

7. To regularly consult with international institutions with an express interest in youth affairs such as the African Union (AU), the United Nations (UN), International Labour Organisation (ILO) and the European Union (EU) on youth trends. Their technical resources could be useful in enhancing the respective operations of the authority.

8. To foster common policies and practices and to promote co-operation, thus:

   a. To co-ordinate the activities of the various government institutions involved in youth matters and to link those activities to the integrated national youth policy.

   b. To develop and implement recommendations relating to any other matters such as conflict, insecurity, skills training, good governance, which may affect the youth.

   c. To develop, implement and manage programmes in areas of investment, economic growth, and entrepreneurship for the survival and development of the youth.

   d. To inculcate in the youth patriotism, peaceful coexistence and entrepreneurial habits and hard work.

e. To coordinate programmes for the spiritual development of the youth.

The Authority should be managed by a management structure comprising:

1. Executive Director
2. Three (3) deputies
   a. Operation/ programmes
   b. Policy
   c. Budgeting and funding
3. Internal auditor
4. Accountant
5. Zonal coordinators
6. Other supporting staff

7. A Board constituted by the heads of all affiliate institutions to the authority, Student Unions, NGO's and selected 'Mmerante-hene'.

On the structure of the board of the authority, the following are recommended:

1. One member from each region, who shall be fit, proper and experienced person in a specific area of need for the functions of the NYA, elected by parliament.

2. Up to five part-time members who are fit for such appointment on account of any qualification, knowledge or experience relating to the functions of the authority, appointed by the President on the advice of a committee of Parliament constituted in terms

of the rules of Parliament, according to the following principles, namely:

    a. Participation by the public in the nomination process;

    b. Transparency and openness; and

    c. The publication of a shortlist of candidates for appointment.

3. The Parliament shall designate two members to serve on the board.

4. The selection of the top management should be done on a competitive basis. The selection process should be handled by a private concern unaffiliated to government in any way.

5. The Minister for Youth and Sports should be a member of the Board as an ordinary member with no executive power.

6. Employers Association, Trades Unions Congress (TUC), Five (5) Representatives of Association of Industries, Representative of The National Vocational Training Institute (NVTI).

## *Term Of Office For Members Of The Board*

1.  The members of the board shall hold office for such fixed term as Parliament may determine at the time of their appointment, but not exceeding five years; provided that Parliament may remove any member from office at any time after consultation with the board if, in their opinion, there are sound reasons for doing so.

2.  Any person whose term of office as a member of the board when expired, may be reappointed.

3.  A member of the board may resign from office by submitting at least three months' prior written notice to Parliament.

4.  The Authority should be allowed to have a maximum of seven (7) committees at a time.

## *Powers, Duties and Functions of Authority*

In addition to any other duties or functions assigned or entrusted to it by Parliament, the Authority shall:

i.  Develop and monitor the implementation of a national youth policy;

ii.  Prioritise national youth issues and initiate youth programmes in accordance with the national youth policy;

iii.  Link the Government to youth organisations and the youth in general in matters pertaining to youth development;

iv.  In consultation with the Government, prioritize

resource allocation to youth affairs;

v.  Assess new needs of and opportunities and challenges for the youth;

vi.  Maintain close liaison with other institutions, bodies or authorities similar to the Authority in order to foster common policies and practices and to promote co-operation in relation to youth affairs;

vii.  Carry out or cause to be carried out such studies concerning youth affairs as may be referred to it by Parliament and the Board.

viii.  On a quarterly basis, report to the Parliament on its activities;

ix.  Monitor and review policies and practices (specific to youth development) of:

    i.  Organs of state at any level;

    ii.  Statutory bodies or functionaries;

    iii.  Public bodies and authorities; and

    iv.  Any other persons, bodies or institutions, with regard to youth matters, and may make any recommendations that the board deems necessary;

    v.  Develop and conduct informative programmes and education programmes, to foster public understanding of matters pertaining to the youth and the role and activities of the board.

x. Evaluate any Act of Parliament or any other law in force at the commencement of the Act establishing the Authority or any law proposed by Parliament or any other legislature after the commencement of this Act, affecting or likely to affect the implementation of the integrated national youth policy and make recommendations to Parliament or such other legislature with regard thereto;

xi. Recommend to Parliament or any other legislature, the adoption of new legislation which would promote the implementation of an integrated national youth policy;

xii. Monitor and review the compliance with international conventions, international covenants and international charters, acceded to or ratified by the Republic, relating to the object of the Authority;

xiii. Prepare and publish reports to Parliament pertaining to any convention, covenant or charter relating to the objects of the Authority;

xiv. Liaise and interact with any organisation which actively promotes youth matters and other sectors of civil society to further the objects of the Authority;

xv. Conduct research or cause research to be conducted to further the objects of the Authority;

xvi. Convene meetings between state departments, including provincial administrations and offices instituted in the provinces, on issues pertaining to the youth; and

xvii.    Consider such recommendations, suggestions and requests concerning youth matters as it may receive from any source;

*(Adopted from the Sierra Leonean Youth Act and Modified)*

## Supporting Institutions

With respect to peace and security, the NYA could work in association with The Ministry of Youth And Sports, Civil Societies, Traditional Authorities, The Police Service, The Armed Forces and Youth Wings of Political Parties and other stakeholders. It should not be just an assembly of collaborating and competing interests.

There should be well defined roles, guidelines for collaboration, and the extent of involvement of each party involved. Suffice to say, these supporting institutions should not be burdened with enormous cost as a result of their participation in this endeavour.

The World Bank through its Youth Enterprise Development Project (YEDP) should be brought in, whilst at the same time synchronising its basic duties.

On entrepreneurship, The NYA should work with the USAID, National Association of Industries, and National Board for Small Scale Industries, the Venture Capital Fund, Enterprise Development Commissions, United Nations Industrial Development Organization (UNIDO), and other relevant organisations.

The issue of governance and democracy is well mentioned as much as craved for by the public and civil society. They are almost a mantra. Civil societies, Non-Governmental Organisations, and political arms of foreign missions could all be selectively approached to help in the inculcation of democratic ideals among the youth.

Institutions such as Regional Technology Transfer Centres (RTTCs), and Regional Appropriate Technology Industrial Service, Integrated Community Centre for Employable Skills (ICCES), Opportunities Industrialisation Centres (OIC), Youth Leadership Institutes, the Private Sector and other organisations including NGOs should increase their capacity and expand their coverage and enrolment of apprentices and ensure that they are well resourced and positioned to assist the NYA in developing the human capacity of the youth.

The Environmental Protection Agency (EPA) could be a strong partner to provide a clean environment and renewable energy and biodiversity. Their role could be in internship for the youth as well as facilitation on training programmes.

# 16

## A Call to Mother Africa and Her Eight Current Cousins

*....Stand up; stand up; stand up ....Don't give up the fight...*

Robert Nesta "Bob" Marley OM

(6 February 1945 – 11 May 1981); A Jamaican Reggae Singer-Songwriter, Musician, and Guitarist

## No Simple Way Out

This is a simple but no ordinary call on all stakeholders to take steps and help solve the youth question across the African continent. But this is not just any call, like a call to help one's family, society and nation. This is a call to stand up for one's self. This is a call which does not require guns and machetes but intellectual and moral weapons without which lasting results can never be secured. This call is made to young persons, nongovernmental organizations, civil society, student unions, young professionals, the political elite and the private businesses. It is a call for all stakeholders to help to put in place structures and a foundation for the economic and cultural empowerment of the Youth.

Young persons should understand that, this call is not a matter of loyalty to a political party. Neither is it a matter of loyalty to fanciful ideological leanings nor affection for heroes or promises. This is a serious matter of loyalty to your interests and aspirations. It does not matter who is delivering your interests; whether brown, white, yellow black, short or tall. The person is your friend as long as he delivers your interests. It is a selfish way of looking at the issue but sometimes, a bit of selfishness could prevent you from falling into the trap of ideological deceptions. Being so young, largely your enthusiasm, innocence and energies are sometimes exploited with little benefit to your general and long term well being.

## African Youth Development Fund

On the larger scale of political institutional muscle, the African Union should not hide behind brilliantly passed legal frameworks. The African Union must step up and see the youth question as a project. By which end the organization should seek to create a fund, say, an initial seven billion US Dollars (USD7Bn) over a period of time for the education, training and development of our youth. The sources of the fund, its administration and disbursement could be worked out at a technical committee level. I would wish to simply add that, this should be spread on need basis across the eight recognized regional economic blocs namely;

1. Arab Maghreb Union (UMA)

2. Common Market for Eastern and Southern Africa (COMESA)

3. Community of Sahel-Saharan States (CEN-SAD)

4. East African Community (EAC)

5. Economic Community of Central African States (ECCAS)

6. Economic Community of West African States (ECOWAS)

7. Intergovernmental Authority on Development (IGAD)

8. Southern Africa Development Community (SADC)

The youth question should be tackled more seriously than any other. It should be seen as a greater version of HIV/ AIDS, Malaria and Poliomyelitis. The African Union should strengthen its youth activities with an independent youth secretariat with a youth coordinator empowered to deliver the mandate. This secretariat should have clear powers, framework of activities and budget among others to make it effective and well positioned to deliver on its mandate.

For the sake of our future, the slow and the uncommitted approach to the Banjul youth action plan should be condemned. There should be renewed vigour to tackle the issue. We need a new force and energy directed at the youth question.

Of course for administrative purposes, the youth secretariat would have to forge a strong network with civil society, regional and national youth authorities. This network should be used to implement, monitor and audit ongoing programmes. It is worth considering Youth Development Centre as a permanent organ of the African Union. This is the time for Africa to stand up for the sake of her youth. The time to leave the conference rooms have long elapsed. It is the time of planting programmes and creating jobs, hope, confidence, a solid future and a prosperous society for the youth. The youth has heard too many words, slogans and phrases. It is time for them to live in the material realities of those words and slogans. From Zambia to Ghana to Nigeria to Kenya and Ethiopia to DR Congo and to South Africa, we must resolve to create a home for our own youth. This is not something beyond us. It is not beyond the ocean or in space. The solution is within us. We must respond to our youth.

Many young persons are choking under the frustrations of their dreams and ambitions. They see darkness all around them with no hope or redemption coming from anywhere. This call goes beyond policy platforms. There are 'a thousand and one' policies around. This is a 'doing-call'. I call on leaders to create the platforms and opportunities for the youth.

Young persons themselves need to abreast themselves with the ongoing issues in their respective countries. These issues should include economic, finance, trade issues, and policy.

Student associations and/or any other political youth movement as it exists should take the centre stage in attempts to
make proposals and push for the right amount of resources
in solving the youth question. And should I say that, these
resources should be in a timely fashion. In the same vein, the
leadership roles of youth movements should include co-operation and coordination of activities with civil societies and other
bodies on the same course. The task of getting the government
to give an ear to the youth question is not going to be easy
considering the number of stakeholders and concerns baffling
most governments. This means that, these stakeholders should
be included in any effort on the table. These stakeholders include private businesses, opposition political parties, trades
unions, traditional institutions and international bodies such
as the African Union and the United Nations.

It is also critical to consult experts for advice on issues which
you might not have mastery over. That is to say, you can make
coherent arguments and appear more persuasive if you have
control of the subject matter you are fighting for. In brief, let
me outline some issues worthy of consideration:

1.  On all issues you are pushing for, there should be
    leadership on your part. Do not allow the government
    or any other institutions to define your needs for
    you. Even in advisory roles, you must be seen as the
    actual proponents of your needs as a youth group. In
    order to guarantee success, there should be a single
    and uniformed leadership. With multiple leaders, the
    'enemy' can easily divide your front.

2. Your demands and/or concerns should be coherent, specific and reasonable. These should be backed by facts.

3. Work with other stakeholders at all times as much as possible. That is to say, build a coalition of stakeholders the government cannot readily ignore. Doing this requires expert skills so there has to be a lot of learning on your feet. The campaign may have to get experts on board in this dimension.

4. Your starting point should be consultations within and outside the youth bracket.

5. Dialogue should be preferred over confrontation.

6. Be prepared to put forward proposals instead of always opposing and raising a storm.

7. Sometimes make minimal concessions and use them as a springboard for your demands. You have to be seen as rational.

8. Be careful not to play into the hands of the opposition political parties or any other interests for that matter.

9. Remember that, as leaders, you are primarily accountable to your constituency, the youth; and when the deed is done, they would judge you on your service to them and not how well you related to the public or the government.

10. Stay the Course. Stay on your message and demands.

11. Break your overall proposals into benchmarks with reasonable timelines.

12. Be focused at all times on your objectives.

13. Give regular feedback to your base. It is important to keep your base informed and supportive. If you break your link with them, your position is likely to be weakened.

14. Use the media to get your message to the public. Press conferences, statements and peaceful demonstrations are permitted.

15. It takes time to get the government to take action so be prepared for the long haul. This calls for discipline and consistency.

16. Remember that, no one would fight for you. People and institutions which genuinely care about the appalling youth situation would not go farther beyond policy and in limited cases, funding. Your success largely depends on you. And let me say that, you are far more equipped with intellectual abilities and resources to access national resources in addressing the youth questions in your respective countries.

17. You must be innovative in all endeavours.

No matter how far you see your dreams, understand that it is within reach. No matter how high up your dream is, note that it is within reach. Build yourselves into armies of scientists, mathematicians, and musicians and nothing could stand in your way....

## *Silver Lining*

The task ahead is daunting but not impossible. Creating seven to ten million jobs a year is no small task for a continents bogged down by weak infrastructure, low capital base, lack of clarity in employment policies and lack of political will to put youth issues on the front burner.

There are interesting pronouncements by wealthy Africans to support the youth cause with seed capital. For instance, Nigeria's Tony O. Olumelu is already preparing to role out major programmes to support Nigerian Youth. His foundation is already accepting proposals for angel funding. Imagine African wealthy individuals joining suit. This coupled with already existing government programmes stands to sow the seed of funding revolution civil society has been calling for, for a long time now. When an observer considers the various African Union and African Development Bank-led programmes, coupled with the respective national programmes, there is a faint line for hope for the continent's youth. At least unlike years past where words have fallen on stubborn ears, this time, these observations could be made:

1.  African leaders have come to accept the youth question as a real challenge which can unravel any ignorant nation

2.  There is the awareness that, action is required

3.  The private sector is willing to enter the ring

4.  Governments have not only talked but taken steps to move ahead with programmes.

5.  There are ongoing programmes for concerted programmes across the continent to pool resources and share risks through the African Union.

6.  Civil society is now bold to highlight the impending youth unemployment Tsunami if African leaders treat the issues as business as usual.

7.  The youth themselves are innovating and have taken the fight to the political elite. Perhaps the most promising sign on the youth question is the spark which has ignited in the eyes of the youth.

    Continue to believe in Africa.

## AU ANTHEM

"Let us all unite and celebrate together
The victories won for our liberation
Let us dedicate ourselves to rise together
To defend our liberty and unity
O Sons and Daughters of Africa
Flesh of the Sun and Flesh of the Sky
Let us make Africa the Tree of Life

Let us all unite and sing together
To uphold the bonds that frame our destiny
Let us dedicate ourselves to fight together
For lasting peace and justice on earth
O Sons and Daughters of Africa
Flesh of the Sun and Flesh of the Sky
Let us make Africa the Tree of Life

Let us all unite and toil together
To give the best we have to Africa
The cradle of mankind and fount of culture
Our pride and hope at break of dawn
O Sons and Daughters of Africa
Flesh of the Sun and Flesh of the Sky
Let us make Africa the Tree of Life"

*Let the African Youth Dream again, because a Great future lies ahead...*

*Africa, Dream Again!*

*African Youth, Dream Beyond the Stars!*

*THE END*

# INDEX

www.ingramcontent.com/pod-product-compliance
Lightning Source LLC
Chambersburg PA
CBHW060242290526
45789CB00001B/156